D1681652

100 SURE-FIRE BUSINESSES YOU CAN START WITH LITTLE OR NO INVESTMENT

100 SURE-FIRE BUSINESSES YOU CAN START WITH LITTLE OR NO INVESTMENT

The Opportunity Guide to Starting Part-Time Businesses and Building Financial Independence

by JEFFREY FEINMAN

₱⋎₱
A Playboy Press Book

Copyright © 1976 by Jeffrey Feinman.

All rights reserved. No part of this book may be reproduced, stored in a retrieval system or transmitted in any form by an electronic, mechanical, photocopying, recording means or otherwise, without prior written permission of the author. Published simultaneously in the United States and Canada by Playboy Press, Chicago, Illinois. Printed in the United States of America.

FIRST EDITION

Playboy and Rabbit Head design are trademarks of Playboy, 919 North Michigan Avenue, Chicago, Illinois 60611 (U.S.A.), Reg. U.S. Pat. Off., marca registrada, marque déposée.

Library of Congress Cataloging in Publication Data

Feinman, Jeffrey.
    100 sure-fire businesses you can start with little or no investment.

    1. Small business. 2. Self-employed.
3. Part-time employment. I. Title.
HD8036.F44   658'.022   75-42349
ISBN 0-87223-458-4

To A. C. Mann
Who Knows About the
Business of Business
and the Business
of Life.

CONTENTS

Introduction: Get Ready for Success	3
1. Professional Cleaning Service	8
2. Home Bakery	10
3. Bookkeeping and Tax Preparation	12
4. House Painting	14
5. Dancing School	16
6. Party Planning Service	18
7. Hauling Service	20
8. Answering Service/Wake-Up Service	22
9. Specialty Newsletter	25
10. Child Care Service	27
11. Special Occasion Movies	29
12. Pet and Plant Care	31
13. Exercise Classes	33
14. Furniture Refinishing	35
15. We-Drive-Your-Car Service	37
16. Art Sales	39
17. Résumés	41
18. Interior Decorating Service	44
19. Sandwich Wagon	47
20. Antique Dealer	49
21. Messenger-Delivery Service	51
22. Booking Agents	54
23. Custom Greeting Cards	56
24. Consignment Shop	59
25. Private Tour Guide	62
26. Specialty Food Selling	65
27. Home Repair Service	67
28. Public Relations	69
29. Business Services	72
30. Music Teacher	75
31. Firewood Supply	77
32. Shut-In Visiting Service	79
33. Salvage-Supply Service	81

34. Small-Business Consultant	84
35. Blade Sharpening	86
36. Backgammon/Bridge/Chess Lessons	88
37. Specialty Auto Repair	90
38. Needlework Decoration	92
39. Household Budget Consultant	94
40. Art Instruction	96
41. Gourmet Cooking Classes	98
42. Exterminator Service	100
43. Self-Defense Instruction	102
44. Foreign Language Translator	104
45. Auto Driving School	106
46. Astrology Readings	108
47. Model Agency	110
48. Craft Instruction	112
49. Vanity Publishing	114
50. TV/Stereo Repair	116
51. Merchant Delivery Service	118
52. Photographer's Representative	120
53. Floor Refinishing	122
54. Printing Broker	124
55. Weight-Loss Classes	126
56. Custom Craft Sales	128
57. Employment Agency	130
58. Portrait Photography	133
59. Pet-Boarding Kennel	136
60. Advertisement and Publication Distribution	138
61. Catering Service	141
62. Nature School	144
63. Calligraphy	147
64. Garage Sale Organizer	150
65. Pottery Selling	153
66. Welcoming Service for Newcomers	156
67. Telephone Solicitor	159
68. Personal Investment Counseling	161
69. Commercial Photography	164
70. Library Research Service	167

71. Fence Installation	170
72. Candy Kitchen	172
73. Collection Agency	174
74. Community Center	176
75. Locksmith	178
76. Business Skills School	180
77. Professional Sound Recording	182
78. Decorative Accessories	184
79. Cosmetic/Fashion Coordinator	186
80. Advertising Specialties	188
81. Landscape Services	190
82. Guidebook Publishing	192
83. Flea Market/Art Show Organizer	194
84. Manufacturer's Representative	196
85. Professional Flower/Plant Service	198
86. Self-Improvement Seminars	200
87. Homemade Jams and Jellies	202
88. Private Tutoring Service	204
89. Recreation Area Concession	206
90. Custom Picture Framing	208
91. Idea Merchant	210
92. Specialty Advertising Agency	212
93. Custom T-Shirt Manufacturing	214
94. Store Window Displays	216
95. Private Brand Vitamin Sales	218
96. Window Washing Service	220
97. Organic Produce Sales	222
98. Jewelry Design and Repair	224
99. Home Service Registry	226
100. Christmas Corporate Gift Service	228

100 SURE-FIRE BUSINESSES YOU CAN START WITH LITTLE OR NO INVESTMENT

Introduction: Get Ready for Success

Horatio Alger is not dead. America is still the land of opportunity. In fact, there were 5000 *new* millionaires last year. But one fact persists. It's almost impossible to make a fortune working for someone else.

This book is a guide to business opportunities. Even if you don't select one of the hundred-plus businesses listed, it will help direct your thinking. Best of all, it will show you that you can start a business with no investment! In fact, most of the businesses listed can be started part-time. You can actually build your business while you keep your job.

The facts are in. Lots of people with no more education, intelligence or skills than you have built huge businesses starting part-time. A West Coast man started selling three-line rubber stamps by mail; his kitchen table company evolved to the giant multimillion-dollar Sunset House. A New York secretary started a part-time employment service to fill her evening hours. Today it's one of the city's largest. I could actually fill an entire book with success stories like these.

Now it's time to give up all your excuses for the job trap. Here's an opportunity for financial independence without risking your job or your life savings. And if you don't make a real fortune, the extra income may at least mean a new car or a summer house. Consider also that the worst thing that can happen is that your business will fail. In that case you've lost only a little spare time and gained a world of experience. There is no question that the knowledge one acquires as an independent businessman is useful in many endeavors.

The only question that remains is "Are you willing to trade some TV time for a chance at financial security?"

How to Select the Right Business for You

Your success will be closely related to selecting a business that's right for you. Much of your current job satisfaction (or dissatisfaction) relates to how your career suits your personal needs. As sad as it sounds, most people spend more time planning a two-week vacation than they spend planning their lives.

All too often one speaks to people about their careers and how "chance" put them in that direction. My neighbor has spent thirty years in the extruded steel tubing business because his college roommate happened to be in that business. The fact is there are no "right" or "wrong" businesses. It is only what is right or wrong for you. The answer comes from spending time with yourself and thinking. Here are some guidelines that will help you.

A. WHAT DO YOU LIKE TO DO?

As silly as it may sound, your favorite hobby may be the key to your financial success. A friend of mine spent long miserable hours at an ad agency job. It provided him little joy. He worked only to earn money to spend vacations scuba diving. In 1968 the agency lost a big account and he was fired. While looking for another job he started a small diving school. You can guess the rest of the story. The business prospered and so did he. Soon he stopped looking for another job. Today he is the most singularly happy person I know. His scuba school now has three junior instructors. In addition to doing what he loves best, he is making money. On the other hand, I wouldn't want to spend forty hours a week scuba diving for a million dollars. I assume you get the point. If you choose what you like to do, your business works for you . . . instead of you for it.

Think about your hobbies and pleasures. There are opportunities for businesses in stamp collecting, photography, cooking and almost any other hobby you might mention. Hugh Hefner seems to have done okay pursuing his favorite hobby.

B. WHERE DO YOU LIKE TO WORK?

Our physical surroundings determine much of our mental state. There are those who think New Yorkers are crazy to live there. And then there are New Yorkers—they believe there is New York and the rest of the world is Bridgeport. Think about location not only in terms of cities. Do you enjoy being inside or outside? Would being a gardener or a nightclub bouncer be more pleasing to you? You'll want to consider locations that would make you happiest.

C. WHAT SKILLS DO YOU HAVE?

Today a good carpenter can make more than the average executive. On the other hand you can't be a part-time decorator if you have no sense of color. Skills are frequently quite different than hobbies. My cousin, a retired government employee, now earns a nice income restoring old furniture. This is a skill that he picked up to save himself money.

However, remember when considering your skills to be careful of conflicts of interest. If your skill is advertising, and you happen to work for an advertising firm, they may take a dim view of your starting a part-time agency.

Make a list of the skills you have. Now, try and fit a business to them.

D. HOW MUCH DO YOU WANT TO MAKE?

Some businesses offer opportunities for you to build them up and then sell them. In other cases you can hire junior people to do the detail work. On the other hand your business may require a skill that cannot be easily taught. That's fine. However, your business decision should relate to potential income. Decide how much money you need and then ask yourself if the type of business you select can ever provide that type of income.

In short, the way to select a business is by "feel." The way you knew that your favorite suit was right was by the way it "felt." You can try on the businesses in this book, mentally, one at a time. The question you want ask is: "Could I see myself doing this?"

Some Basics to Consider

This book assumes at least a common-sense knowledge of running a business. However, it may be worthwhile to review some basics.

A. SETTING UP

You'll probably want your business to be a single proprietorship. You can examine the tax advantages and record-keeping advantages in any basic accounting book. However, a corporation offers the distinct advantage of limited liability. That is, if your business may involve potentially large transactions or indebtedness, you should consider that you are *personally* liable unless you've had the foresight to incorporate.

One person you'll want to contact early in your planning is your insurance agent. Fire and theft insurance are basic. But product liability and other types of coverage may be required.

B. BOOKKEEPING

No matter how small your new venture, Uncle Sam has the right to look in on your books. The problems really start if you don't have a set of books. And the IRS should be among the top ten on the list of people you don't want to get angry. Don't let record-keeping scare you off. Any stationery store can provide a simple bookkeeping system. It's unbelievable how many seasoned executives think they can get away with keeping the numbers in their head.

C. TAXES

There are numerous tax advantages to your new small business. You may be able to write off part of your mortgage payments or part of your travel costs. The minimal fee a good C.P.A. charges is well worth the cost. See him early, when you are getting started.

D. LICENSES AND PERMITS

Certain of the businesses listed in this book may require a license or permit. This varies widely from state to state and community to community. To find out, simply contact the county clerk's office in your city. In almost every case this is simply a matter of filling out a short application and paying a license fee. This can usually be done in a few minutes (without a lawyer) and the fees are seldom over $20. If you have any doubts about the legal ramifications (on a federal, state or local level), a short consultation with an attorney will be inexpensive and free your mind. There are *no* businesses included that require extensive training, state board examinations or expensive license requirements.

Let's Go

It's all out there waiting for you. Sit down and pick out a business that will work for you. Stay away from the gloom and doom and depression storytellers. This is a time filled with opportunity. It's probably best said by the following quote from an anonymous sage:

> Nothing in the world can take the place of persistence. Talent will not; nothing is more common than unsuccessful men with talent. . . . Genius will not; unrewarded genius is almost a proverb. Education will not; the world is full of educated derelicts. Persistence and determination alone are omnipotent. The slogan "Press on" has solved, and always will solve.

1 · *Professional Cleaning Service*

One of the steadiest service businesses going is also one of the most invisible. If you work in an office or store you're probably used to coming in every morning and seeing clean carpets, empty ashtrays and freshly mopped woodwork. In fact, most stores and offices would be pretty dreary places to work if you *didn't* see them sparkling clean every day.

Starting your own professional cleaning service is easier than starting many other kinds of businesses precisely because it is invisible. That is, the business is performed at night. While you are in the process of putting your cleaning service together you can maintain your day job until your income from the cleaning business is big enough to support you by itself.

The equipment you need to start this business is minimal: a good vacuum cleaner, mops, brooms, cleaning cloths, sponges, buckets and a few different types of detergents and grease-cutting fluids. If this list sounds familiar, it should. These are the same cleaning tools found in almost every household, and there's no reason you can't use what you already probably own—at least for starters.

There are several ways to acquire customers: small ads in your local newspaper, a listing in the Yellow Pages (under "Janitor Service" and/or "House Cleaning"), printed circulars. But the most effective way to get customers is through personal solicitation. Always remember that you are offering a *service*, and that means servicing your clients as well as their places of business.

Start by calling people you know who either work at or own their own retail store, suite of offices, or restaurant; even call affluent homeowners. Make appointments to see these people late in the day or even during your lunch hour. And when you do get to see them, come prepared to discuss price specifically. Since this kind of business requires an investment of time more than anything else, it can be very tricky to price properly.

There's only one good way to find out how long it takes to clean an office thoroughly. Do it yourself. You might try working nights for a while for another cleaning service, as an employee. Or just time yourself carefully while cleaning one or more rooms in your own house or apartment. You pricing will be based on the hourly pay rate to a small crew of workers you will hire (or yourself if you participate in the actual cleaning) plus your cost for cleaning materials and depreciation on your cleaning tools, and your profit. For example, if you figure it will take one person two and a half hours to clean a suite of eight offices, *your* costs will be: $6.25 for employee's salary (at $2.50 per hour), $1.50 for supplies and $1 for "overhead" (advertising bookkeeping, etc.). That comes to $8.75. For twenty working days a month your costs amount to $180. You charge your customer between $250 and $300 and your net profit runs between $70 and $120.

When soliciting customers, your objective is to sign them up to a six-month or year contract, payable monthly. You might offer a one-month trial, with an option to extend, to give customers a reasonably risk-free way to try your service.

One of the attractive features about starting this kind of business is that the work is done at night. You could do the whole thing yourself, without any employees, during the trial period, and still keep your day job. When you are ready to hire people you have a rich source of employees in college students who want part-time work after classes, as well as men and women who want to supplement their incomes but can only work at night.

As you can see from our example of costs, with contracts for ten or twelve offices, stores or restaurants, you can easily net more than $1000 a month. The growth potential for this business is obvious. The points to remember are to use good personal selling techniques and to carefully price each job before committing yourself to a months-long contract. As your business grows you'll be in a position to bid on major cleaning contracts for large companies, each one alone being worth thousands in profit.

2 · Home Bakery

We all know someone who is noted for baking delicious tollhouse cookies or mouth-watering blueberry pie. You yourself may be the proud cook people talk about after a delicious dessert has been served at one of your dinner parties. And there's certainly no argument when we compare homemade baked goods to the commercial stuff available in supermarkets. Well, then, what about producing your baked specialty for sale in your community? It can be done, very successfully, but there are several considerations.

Bear in mind, first of all, that baking bread, cake, pie or cookies for a special occasion can be great fun. But to make money in a home baking business you have to bake your specialty many times a week, over and over again. In other words, you must first come to grips with the fact that "commercial" baking is work, good and lucrative work, but quite different from once-in-a-while party baking.

Starting a home bakery business is relatively easy. Let's say your specialty is a delicious, rich cheesecake. The first step, before soliciting one order, is to figure out exactly how much one cake costs you. This means calculating *every* ingredient, including the fraction of a pound of butter you use to grease your cakepan and the cost of power to bake your cake. Breaking costs down to the price per egg and the price per cup of flour is more complicated than it seems at first. And once you've figured the exact cost of all the ingredients you'll probably be surprised to find out how expensive your cake has been, not counting your labor. Now take the cost you've arrived at and double it. That will be your selling price. Don't be shocked to discover that your selling price for one cheesecake could be as high as $6 or more, and don't be discouraged. People expect to pay more for homemade baked goods because there is just no commercial product that can compare.

Your objective in selling your baked goods is to line up as many regular customers as possible. This means your primary effort should be directed to local restaurants, delicatessens and small groceries. The idea here is to line up customers who will take a weekly quantity of your product, as opposed to individuals who buy one cake at a time for a special occasion. Once you've established your "institutional" buyers then there will be time to think about advertising for direct sales to consumers.

Visit restaurants and stores with your samples in hand. You will get more attention from the owner of the establishment if you visit during the quieter hours of the day (not at mealtime). Offer to leave one of your products as a test. If your cake is as good as you've been told by family and friends you should get a large order when you call back in a few days. Once your baked product has become a regular feature in several outlets, the biggest problem you'll probably be facing is how to keep up with the demand.

At some point you will have to come to a decision about how large you want your business to be. The danger, of course, is the loss of home-baked quality. Don't be tempted to "cheat" on the ingredients, even slightly, because discerning customers will catch on soon enough.

With a modest start in your own kitchen, using the cost structure outlined above, you should be able to earn $50 a week or more after paying for ingredients. (Collect from your customers at the time of delivery.) When you get to the point of adding commercial ovens and a staff of helpers your income could jump to $500 a week or more.

A final suggestion: Stick to baked goods you know are proven winners. If your specialty is a melt-in-your-mouth chocolate layer cake, don't assume that anything you turn out of your oven will be an automatic best seller. Venture into related baked goods cautiously and only after careful taste-testing.

3 · Bookkeeping and Tax Preparation

One of the annoying aspects of running any small business is the difficulty of finding an accountant who doesn't cost an arm and a leg. Most people who own and run their own retail stores or service businesses are capable of maintaining their own financial books, but when quarterly tax time comes it's as if these people were suddenly asked to speak a foreign language for the first time in their lives.

If you have had any accounting experience, you are probably qualified to perform this service, especially if you are acquainted with more than one system of bookkeeping. Although most of your prospective clients will maintain their own weekly bookkeeping, you can offer this additional service to those who want it.

To sell your service you should make a minimum investment in a Yellow Pages listing under "Tax Return Preparation" (or "Bookkeeping Service"), as well as placing small classified ads in your local newspaper. Personal visits to community retailers are helpful, especially if you have the time to strike up a conversation, mention what business you are in and leave a business card for the retailer's reference.

A natural outgrowth of this business is, of course, individual tax return preparation. Most owners of businesses tend to use their business tax preparer for their personal returns. Although personal tax preparation is a seasonal business, it can be extremely lucrative. H&R Bloch has grown to become a multimillion-dollar business on this "seasonal" work alone.

For your business clients you should set your rates so that you make at least $15 an hour. Since quarterly tax returns will come due for different clients at different times (because they are not all on the same fiscal schedule), you can plan your time accordingly. To keep your rates competitive, check the competition. Call a few of the bookkeeping or tax preparation services listed in the Yellow Pages and ask them their rates as if you were a potential client.

Your goal in this business is to establish a growing list of clients. But even as a solo practitioner, handling only the number of clients you can service by yourself, your income can easily top $30,000 a year. If you wish to grow larger, you could end up supervising an office full of trained staff members. Your initial investment to start this business need be nothing more than the cost of a supply of business cards and letterheads.

4 · House Painting

Here is one business in which little training is required. The skill required to paint a house, inside or out, is mainly a combination of neatness and speed. Since the labor is rudimentary, it means you'll also have an easier time hiring help, such as energetic college students. The supplies you need to start your business are also rudimentary: brushes, rollers and pans, paint thinner and ladders, and possibly a paint sprayer (this can be rented).

Your advertising should consist of a listing in the Yellow Pages and a small ad in local newspapers. If your first ad does not draw enough responses to pay for the printer's ink, don't automatically assume it's going to take you months to get your first painting job. Rewrite your ad. Check the ads from other painting services and find the unique quality you want to promote in your service. For instance, if another painter says "Known County-Wide For 38 Years of Quality Service" in his ad, you obviously cannot compete with that kind of claim. But you can develop some aspect of your own service that can create almost as much credibility and attention. You can say something like, "Free *Written* Estimate Within 24 Hours, Every Paint Job Guaranteed For 2 Full Years." These are services that most reputable painters offer, but few advertise.

Regardless, you can't sit at home and just wait for your advertising to bring customers calling—especially with a service that is usually offered by many people in the same town. As with any business that's going to succeed you have to go out there and drum up business personally. Call professional people you know and ask if their offices could use a professional-quality inexpensive paint job. Leave your business card wherever it will be seen, including paint stores willing to give them out. You *will* get requests for estimates.

Although the painting itself is not beyond the skill of most people, there is an aspect of a painting service that can make or break your business on one or two jobs. Before you deliver your first estimate to a potential customer, learn some of the intricacies of judging a job. That means knowing exactly how much paint you'll need for the job and how much time to calculate to complete it. If you forgot to count the windows in a certain room, you might find yourself needing an extra two days to paint windowpanes. One six- or eight-paned window takes as much time as an interior wall.

One young painting contractor in Connecticut saw his business triple in one year because he experimented and found a way to estimate by means of a formula. His estimates were almost always among the lowest submitted, yet he never ran short of paint or misjudged the time necessary to finish a job. You don't have to develop your own formula but you do have to apply a good dose of common sense to your estimating.

There are two good places for the beginning paint contractor to go for information. The first is a paint wholesaler who, in the interest of selling more of his product, will give you sound help in figuring "spread," the amount of paint needed to cover a given area, and advice on the quality of different kinds of paint. The other place to go is to another painting contractor, preferably as an employee. Unfortunately, there's just no better way to learn than to do. What you pick up in one or two months of working for a contractor is probably worth more than a dozen books on the subject.

When putting together your figures for an estimate, take your wholesale price for the paint and add 30 percent to that. Retail paint stores add about 40 percent, so you can offer an advantage to your customer and still make a profit. Your labor costs should be based on a minimum wage for your unskilled help, plus 50 percent as your profit. If you're painting someone's apartment and you've calculated that you'll need nine gallons of paint and it will take two painters four days to do the job, your estimate would be arrived at like this:

9 gallons (wholesale) @ $5.65	=	$ 50.85
30% profit	=	15.26
2 painters @ $2.50/hr. for 32 hrs.	=	160.00
50% profit on labor	=	80.00
TOTAL FOR JOB		$306.11

As you can calculate, your profit comes to nearly $100, and that is a modest-sized paint job. Exterior painting is usually more. The growth potential is strong for this highly competitive business.

5 · Dancing School

There are as many opportunities for a successful dancing school as there are ways to dance. And the funny thing is, you don't have to be a brilliant dancer to be a successful dancing school owner and/or teacher. Whether it's square dancing, ballet, ballroom or contemporary rock dancing, there are great numbers of people who want to learn. Of course, your own preference and the most popular dances in your community will pretty much dictate the kind of dancing you choose to emphasize in your school. Regardless of the type of dance, the methods for getting it together are the same.

If you can, hold classes in your own home. If you don't have enough room but one of your students does, offer free lessons for that student in exchange for the use of a basement (or any large room). For most types of dance instruction you won't need any props. The exceptions are ballet or jazz dancing, in which case a large mirror and a dance bar are a necessity. If free space is not available, the next best situation would be some place like a local Y or church. In exchange for the hall (and that group's sponsorship) you usually give a percentage of your tuition receipts. The amount of the percentage is negotiable, but should never exceed 50 percent.

To set up a class, begin by writing a clear, concise brochure that outlines the complete schedule and prices. This brochure will be your major selling piece, the piece you send to every interested person. Then put together a small classified ad soliciting inquiries: "CHILDREN'S BALLET SCHOOL. New Classes Start February 1. Call 866-3554 For Complete Information."

Don't stop at a classified ad. If it's a children's ballet school you're starting, call your friends who have children and sell them on the school. Put notices up on nursery school bulletin boards, at day care centers, at youth centers. Leave your business cards at children's clothing stores and toy shops.

Your basic teaching tools will be a phonograph (a portable is sufficient) and a generous supply of records. You should figure your rates so that you end up with approximately $20 to $25 an hour gross profit. This means a class of ten would be charged about $2.50

per person per lesson. Try to get your dance instruction customers to agree to a series of lessons, say one lesson a week for six to ten weeks. (Any series longer than ten weeks is stretching it.) Of course, if you are teaching smaller classes, customers will pay more and will be getting more individualized attention for their money.

Once you have gotten a series of classes under way, it's not difficult to see how quickly your school can grow. You can hire other instructors for an hourly salary, or even a percentage of the tuition the instructor generates. Within a relatively short time you could find yourself with a thriving, growing business that could produce a net income of $20,000 a year on up.

6 · Party Planning Service

More than most businesses, party planning depends on establishing a good personal relationship with your customers. Although good party planners will undoubtedly get repeat business from many customers, most festive occasions you organize will be one-shot affairs, like a wedding or bar mitzvah or "sweet sixteen" party. You'll have one crack at satisfying a client you may never serve again, but that client could be responsible for getting you another dozen customers. The long-term success of your business will ultimately depend on word-of-mouth recommendations. Organize one very successful bar mitzvah celebration and you could find yourself deluged with calls from parents of twelve-year-old boys who heard you were responsible for that terrific party everyone loved so much.

The ingredients of a successful party planner are good organization, imagination and an ability to understand your client's desires, both stated and unstated. Your selling tools will be a Yellow Pages listing, a specific classified ad and a desk and telephone in your home. Your classified ad should stress the different kinds of parties you can plan, by name (children's birthdays, engagement parties, weddings, communion celebrations, Halloween parties, office parties, Christmas parties and so on). You should also establish contacts with catering houses, musical groups and specialists in young children's entertainment, like free-lance magicians and clowns.

When you have your first meeting with a client, be friendly and informal but be sure to get a list of facts you will need to make intelligent proposals. Find out the kind of people who will be attending the party, what the occasion is, the age of the guests, how many will be attending, where the party will be held and, most important, how much money per guest your client wants to spend. Your fee should be based on a percentage of the cost of the party, say 15 percent. If your client is throwing a bash for fifty people and is willing to spend $7 per person, or a total of $350, you should be able to bring the party in for about $295, leaving a fee of $55 for you.

In addition to consulting with your client to plan the party, you will be responsible for hiring the caterer and entertainers, making sure they provide everything you need, and you will probably have to attend the party to make sure everything runs smoothly. If the total cost for the party is $350, get from one-third to one-half of that amount several weeks before the party and the balance immediately after the party (the same day). Your suppliers will want to be paid quickly and you should not put yourself in a position of paying any expenses out of your own pocket.

If you enjoy entertaining, this business can be as much fun as it is lucrative. The possibilities for creating exciting parties are practically unlimited. For children's birthdays you can organize excursions to amusement parks, skating rinks, swimming pools and the like. Weather permitting, you can even put together a mini-circus right in a youngster's own back yard.

Adult parties with exciting themes, election-night get-togethers, retirement dinners, teas for ladies' groups—you could be called on to plan any or all of these. If you can become familiar with social committees in different companies, you could develop a number of institutional accounts that will use your service on a regular basis. You might explain to prospective clients that your contacts with caterers and others who give you professional discounts mean that you can throw a first-rate party, from invitations to good-night snacks, for no more than the host would normally pay. And with your professional service the host can *enjoy* the party without worrying about any of the details.

7 · Hauling Service

Any business that's easy to start is bound to attract a number of enterprising, hard-working "independents." Because a hauling service can be started with as little as an old station wagon and a willingness to get your hands dirty, you can expect that such a service is a pretty competitive business. So, to succeed in this low-investment service business you have to offer something that will attract customers to you rather than others who may have better equipment, or a long-established list of customers.

To get customers in your new business you have to be willing to work harder than the competition. Start with a classified ad in your local paper that says something to the effect of, "Efficient Low-Cost Hauling. Our Prices Are The Best In Town. No Job Too Small. Call 764-9823 for immediate FREE estimate."

If the job you get requires a vehicle larger than a station wagon (although you'll be surprised how much you can fit in a wagon), you can rent a larger vehicle from Ryder or U-Haul (every town has at least one rental service). But you don't have to rent an expensive truck for bigger hauling jobs. You can rent, or even build, a small trailer! No one really cares how you haul away whatever junk they want to get rid of, and no one will be checking the paint job on the vehicle you use. The point is to keep your costs as low as possible.

Helpers in the hauling business are easy to come by. High school students or virtually anyone who wants a few hours work are likely candidates at the going minimum wage. In addition to a classified ad, your promotion costs should be limited to business cards, a listing in the Yellow Pages (under "Trucking" or "Hauling") and a neatly lettered sign, with a telephone number, on your vehicle. Make a habit of talking up your service whenever possible, and leave cards with prospective customers and others who can distribute them casually.

Your rates should be stated to customers in terms of a flat fee (usually never less than $15, no matter how small the job). When figuring your fee calculate the time necessary for the job, the salary to your helper, if needed, gas, wear and tear on your vehicle, rental

charges for a vehicle and any dumping fees you may have to fork over at the town dump. Then take those basic "costs" and add another 50 percent as your profit. With reasonably steady work you could be making a profit of $200 a week in a relatively short time. Collect your fee after you load your vehicle, before you leave your customer's property. You should have little difficulty doing this since your job is done at that point, at least as far as the customer is concerned.

As your business grows, you can acquire your own larger vehicles (or even lease them on a long-term basis). You can easily branch out into the moving business, and even the salvage business (by saving and restoring broken items that others have hired you to discard).

8 · Answering Service/Wake-Up Service

Despite the appearance of low-cost recorded answering devices, there is still a thriving demand for answering services featuring a live person on the other end of the line. If you have ever called someone who used a recording device for an answering service you probably know why. People just cannot carry on a satisfactory conversation with a machine. For doctors in particular the recorded message answering service was never an acceptable substitute. But now most small, one-person businesses that rely on telephone calls from potential customers realize the value of having a person answer the phone who can respond immediately to the caller's particular needs.

Basically the way an answering service works is quite simple. It is an extension of your client's telephone with the number ringing on your switchboard at the same time it rings on his telephone. After three or more rings the answering service picks up and says, for instance, "Dr. Thompson's office," and the person is answered just as if he had actually reached Dr. Thompson's office. The service takes a message and either gets in touch with the client immediately or reports with a series of messages at one time. For doctors this service is quite indispensable. For other professionals and small businesses the answering service acts as their office switchboard.

This is the kind of business you can run from one room in your home. For a fee, the telephone company simply runs lines into a switchboard they install for this purpose. In some states the telephone company requires you to have a minimum number of customers before they will set up this equipment. You will have to lay out an advance sum of money when the equipment is installed, just as you did when you were having new telephones installed in your house. You should check your telephone company's business office for specific rates.

To get customers for your service you should have a small listing in the Yellow Pages. You should also prepare a small brochure for specific customers, listing your rates. To start you should try to limit yourself to handling telephone messages during the business day. Anything approaching an 18- or 24-hour service will require a trained staff. The best training you can get for this kind of business is to work as an operator for someone else's answering service.

Bear in mind that when you try to solicit customers, especially doctors, you will be dealing with prospective clients who already employ an answering service. You will have to approach these prospective clients with the goal of winning them away rather than selling them on the service. The best way to win over clients is obviously to offer features that other services do not. Price is the most competitive feature of an answering service. Your pricing must be figured accurately, which you can only do once you have arrived at detailed rates with the telephone company business office. If you are in an area that has a limited number of message units for a flat rate with an additional charge for additional calls, you will have to base your pricing accordingly.

Stress in your brochure that your service will be tailored exactly to the needs of the client. Solicit customers who may not be using an answering service now possibly because they didn't realize how helpful it could be to them. A local TV repair shop may be owner-operated. The owner may be in the shop much of the time but involved in work that does not allow him to answer the phone easily. Stress that you not only take messages but also make appointments and deal with TV repair customers, almost as if you were in the shop.

If the money necessary to run telephone lines into your home to a switchboard is beyond your means right now, there is another way to start your own answering service more modestly You can have your client list *your* telephone number as an alternative if there is no answer at the telephone listed for his place of business. In this way, you can avoid the immediate expense of sophisticated telephone equipment and still offer many of the same advantages to your customers. This means, of course, that you will have to start with a smaller nucleus of clients since you must leave your telephone reasonably free to receive as many messages as possible. For this more modest beginning consider having one telephone to receive telephone calls and another telephone to deliver messages. This way, of course, one phone remains free for incoming calls at all times.

Take the trouble to visit prospective clients personally. They will appreciate the attention and you will be much better equipped to discuss a client's needs if you can also see the setting in which your client works.

To supplement the income from your service, you can offer a wake-up service. Your fee for waking people nicely by telephone twenty times a month will be approximately $6 to $8 dollars a month, depending on local telephone rates.

The telephone is a valuable moneymaking instrument. It's a particularly good business for people who must stay at home during the day, such as a parent with a young child or a handicapped individual. The versatility of the telephone means that you could offer additional services to your clients, such as reminders by telephone for important birthdays, anniversaries and other occasions. You might also offer a telephone solicitation business to your answering service clients.

9 · Specialty Newsletter

A fellow by the name of Michael Holmes spent a great deal of time with his hobby of restoring antique stringed instruments. He also enjoyed playing the guitar and banjo, and visiting Blue Grass music festivals during his vacations. When he lost his job several years ago, he decided to take a crack at turning his hobby into a money-making profession. He decided to publish a newsletter for those who collected and restored antique stringed instruments.

He put together his specialty newsletter business with methods that generally apply to any kind of newsletter you wish to produce. Of course, the first thing he did was choose a subject with which he was already quite familiar, and you should do the same thing. Whether your interest is sports, the stock market, music, or television watching, the methods for selling information are the same. (One woman, an avid soap opera watcher, actually started a newsletter in which she summarized the plots of soap operas appearing each day on the major networks. For those, like her, who are avid soap opera fans she provided the service of keeping viewers up to date about plot developments for the top soap opera programs.)

But whatever your area of interest, you must start by finding an audience to whom you can mail letters or brochures stating the kind of information you want to sell.

Most specialty newsletters will appeal to a select audience of no more than a few thousand. The idea is to find mailing lists from commercial list brokers consisting of people who share your interest. Or, you can place small ads in magazines which would appeal to the kind of people you want to reach. You then solicit subscriptions for a monthly or even bimonthly newsletter of about four to six pages. The gathering of subscribers will be your greatest expense.

Assuming, of course, you can put together the specialized information necessary (which our woman soap opera fan did simply by paying very close attention to three TV sets at one time) your expenses are minimal. The newsletter itself is usually typewritten on 8½ x 11 paper and can be reproduced on a mimeograph machine or with inexpensive offset printing. Your cost for mailing and printing will probably not exceed 20¢ for each issue you mail out. Depending on how specialized your newsletter is, you can charge anywhere from $10 to $50 or more for a year's subscription.

Mailing lists of potential subscribers can be acquired through list brokers at a cost of about $30 per thousand names. Look under "Mailing Lists" in the Yellow Pages of your city's telephone directory. As you can quickly calculate, if you are able to get $10 for twelve issues of a newsletter (which costs you about $2.40 to produce in a year) your profit potential is substantial. Your newsletter will be successful if you offer subscribers information they want but cannot easily get otherwise.

Many entrepreneurs who started newsletters from a corner of a room in their homes have seen their projects blossom into very lucrative businesses, grossing as much as $100,000 or more per year.

10 · Child Care Service

As the number of working women in this country has grown in recent years, so has the need for a place to leave young children during the day. The government has helped by providing day care centers in many areas, but these are really available only to a relatively small number of working mothers. To fill this service that is not available to so many working mothers, you can create a day care center in your home or apartment with almost no investment.

The first thing you should do, before even soliciting working mothers, is to check your local education department for licensing requirements and insurance needs. You should, by yourself, be able to care for up to ten children at one time.

To keep the children happy and occupied you should have a supply of children's books and games, and, if possible, outdoor equipment like slides and swings. Small classified ads promoting your service in the local newspaper should be enough to draw a number of inquiries. The usual charge for this kind of service comes to about $1 to $1.50 per hour per child. This means you could gross as much as $15 an hour with almost no overhead. Working mothers will be expected to bring their children to your home in the morning and pick them up in the afternoon. You may provide lunch for the children, but many small, private day care centers ask that children bring their own lunch, and this has not proven to be too much of a hardship for the working mothers.

Once you have a "full house," you will be in a position to earn anywhere from $250 a week on up. Of course, you have to like children and children will have to like you. It is not easy to supervise a group of children. You will probably be tired at the end of the day.

Your business could grow from a home day care center into a larger number of centers with a staff that you train. The idea is to keep your fees reasonable enough so that it is worthwhile for a working mother to pay to have her child watched and still earn money from her own work.

An important feature of your business, especially at the beginning, should be a willingness on your part to watch children for as little as an hour or two at an hourly rate of $1.50 while the parent shops or keeps an appointment. Don't commit yourself only to full-day watching of children. Be flexible, be understanding, and make the environment you are creating one which children will want to return to whenever their parents must go out.

Bear in mind, of course, we are talking about preschool children, so that it will not be necessary for you to offer any kind of classroom instruction. The degree of versatility you are ready to offer will really depend on how much energy you wish to put into the center itself.

11 · Special Occasion Movies

With the quality of reasonably priced 8mm cameras and film being manufactured today, it is now quite easy to produce a fifteen- to twenty-minute film of virtually any special occasion, from a wedding to a bar mitzvah to an engagement party or children's birthday party. And you don't have to be an Otto Preminger to produce a film that will entertain as well as become a cherished memory of any important celebration. Your basic supplies for a finished fifteen- to twenty-minute movie will include eight to ten rolls of 8mm film (a total of about thirty-two to forty minutes of film which you will edit down to twenty minutes or less). In addition, of course, you'll need a decent 8mm camera, which you may already own, an inexpensive film editor (which can be purchased for as little as $15) and floodlights.

Begin by writing a simple film script before you actually start shooting. If you are producing a film of someone's wedding, for instance, make sure you list all of the scenes you want to capture on film, such as the bride before the ceremony, the maid of honor and ushers preparing for the wedding, the actual ceremony, the tossing of rice, and the party afterward. Just be sure you include as many people as possible in the film, especially the family of the bride and groom.

You might also prepare carefully lettered titles to lead into the film, which will add a sophisticated touch to your production. Your actual costs to produce a twenty-minute film, using eight rolls of film, should be about $40 to $50. You should charge anywhere from $100 to $200 for this film, which will compare favorably with professional still photographs the hosts might have contracted for, yet will provide a much more enjoyable memento of the occasion.

To solicit customers for this unique service, check through your local newspapers for engagement announcements in particular. You should also run a small classified ad that says something to the effect of: "Now capture in movies every moment of your most cherished celebrations." Telephone those people whose engagements have been announced, and set up a personal meeting to discuss the service you can offer.

Be flexible enough to make a shorter or longer film, depending on the needs of your client. This is one kind of business in which word-of-mouth advertising will play a more important role than printed advertising. Get your basic film and developing from a professional photo supply house if possible. Emphasize that you are a professional and will be a regular customer for this supply house.

As a sideline to this film production business you might even be in a position to sell movie projectors and screens to your clients at reduced prices. Once you have contracted for your first job, have a duplicate print made of your film so that you can show this feature as a sample of your work. It will be your most powerful selling tool.

12 · Pet and Plant Care

When a family wants to vacation for a week, or even a few days, one of the problems is who will take care of the house. Namely, who will feed the pets, water the plants, pick up the mail, and who will make sure that the house stays generally in one piece?

Two women who love animals realized this was a problem for many families, so they started a business in which they visit a customer's house twice a day to feed the animals, pick up the mail and look after things. In exchange for this service they charge between $2 and $3 dollars a visit.

You could start the same kind of business right out of your own house for no investment whatsoever, except a small classified ad in the newspaper. If you figure that it takes about fifteen minutes to a half hour to drive to someone's house, feed the pets and let the dog out to play, you can average from $4 to $10 an hour for your service.

The advantage for your customers is obvious. There is a responsible person checking their house every day, the pets do not have to be put into an expensive boarding kennel, the plants will not die from lack of water, mail and newspapers will be picked up so that would-be burglars will not have any idea that no one is home. So, for about $4 to $6 a day, your customer can go on a vacation with the secure feeling that everything is being looked after.

In reality you are offering much more than just pet and plant care. You are providing home security. You will find that after you have served a few clients, word-of-mouth advertising will be your most valuable advertising. And it will be free.

The two women mentioned above had full-time jobs when they began this service. But within a matter of months they had so many clients that they were able to give up their full-time jobs and devote all their time to the work they liked best, namely, taking care of people's homes and pets. Their customers are required to leave enough pet food in the house to take care of the animals throughout the vacation. If you buy food for the pets, this should be added to your fee. You will not have any billing problems if you ask for payment before the customer leaves for vacation, or, at the latest, as soon as your customer returns.

Your expenses are really limited only to the gasoline needed to drive your car to the customer's house. If your service will extend over a period of weeks, as it will for customers who go away on longer vacations, you should advise your clients to notify the police that the pet and plant care service will be visiting their home daily.

As your business grows, you will find that you hire others to service additional homes. You can figure that with an earning rate of $4 to $10 an hour, you could be drawing an income from this business of anywhere from $150 a week to $400 a week. And that is with almost no expenses to you. Stress to your prospective clients that your service is performed by mature people who have a great deal of experience in caring for pets. Your service should be much preferred to the services of a neighborhood youngster. Most people will gladly pay as much as $6 a day to have their homes looked after in this manner, especially if they have more than one pet. Rates in boarding kennels are usually $5 a day per pet, and this places a pet in an unfamiliar setting which cannot compare to being at home. The prerequisite, of course, is that you enjoy animals and that you are able to give them the affection that is missing while their owners are away.

13 · Exercise Classes

Regular exercise is something every overweight adult knows is good for him or her, but is difficult if not impossible to perform alone. The discipline necessary for regular exercising is just something most people don't have. The alternative in most communities is an exercise salon, which can be quite expensive.

You can start your own exercise classes right in your home with a very small investment in equipment and at prices that will compete favorably with the franchised commercial exercise salons. Group exercising seems to be easier, and most people who want to exercise find that they are much more conscientious when they can exercise with a group that wants the same benefits.

To begin with, you should place a classified ad in your local newspaper emphasizing the joy of exercise in small classes at rates that everyone can afford. You only need a basement playroom or any large, clear area in your home to set up your classes. If you don't have the space available, consider going to a local "Y" or church organization, and offer to run exercise classes in their facilities while paying them a percentage of your fees.

You do not have to be a physical culture expert to run an exercise class, but you do have to be in reasonably good shape. There are virtually dozens of books on exercising, any one of which will give you the basics of what exercises to perform for weight loss and good health. You learn quickly how long to run each exercise, as well as which exercises are the best, depending on the physical condition of your class. When putting together your curriculum, make sure each exercise is interesting and not too long. Keep each group limited to no more than ten or fifteen people.

Set up your exercise schedule as a series of once-a-week classes running for six to ten weeks. Any series of longer duration will tend to discourage people, who usually don't want to commit themselves for more than a period of about three months at a time. Because of your low "overhead" you will compete favorably with the commercial salons. You should charge between $2 and $4 per class per student, and each class should run about forty-five minutes to an hour. If you have a class with ten participants, your gross income can be as much as $20 an hour or more. If you are using someone else's facility you will have to deduct whatever percentage you have agreed to pay for the use of that facility. Under no circumstances should you be paying more than 50 percent of your income for the use of someone else's room.

In addition to a classified ad, you should prepare a small poster which can be done on a 8½ x 11 paper, mimeographed, announcing your classes and giving your telephone number. You should post these flyers wherever you will be given the space, such as local retail stores, church and "Y" bulletin boards, even on local supermarket bulletin boards which are usually set aside for community announcements.

If you are able to run four, five or six classes a day, which is pretty demanding physically, you will be able to clear as much as $200 a week or more. Your time initially will be spent in getting customers for your classes. Once you have put together as many groups as you can comfortably service over a six- to ten-week period, you might be in a position to hire additional staff and have several classes running at the same time. This is how many commercial franchise exercise salons began.

You do not need any equipment, except mats for the floor. You do not have to have exotic exercise machinery since most of your exercising will be done while standing or lying down.

When selling your exercise classes you should emphasize the weight-loss nature of the classes. As a supplement to the classes you can print, by mimeograph or offset, suggested diets and other healthful, nutritional suggestions for your clients. As you get into this business, sell the fact that many of your clients have lost weight while taking your classes. If possible take before-and-after pictures to use for promotional purposes. The only equipment your students will need is a leotard or loose fitting clothing that allows mobility.

Before actually holding your first class, be sure to check with your insurance agent on your needs for liability insurance. You cannot be sure that a student who signs up for the class does not have some hidden ailment of which you are unaware. For the small sum it will require, it is far better to be safe and have whatever insurance will cover you satisfactorily.

14 · Furniture Refinishing

In times of economic stress, people are always looking for ways to make old things last longer. This is especially true of furniture, some of the most expensive items to replace in anyone's household. Furniture refinishing is not difficult work, but most people prefer not to do it themselves.

Refinishing is a matter of sanding down or removing old finish carefully and smoothly, then restaining or repainting the furniture. It does require some open space, preferably a garage or basement with plenty of ventilation. You will be using solvents frequently to strip furniture, as well as as thin paint and stain, and you must have enough air coming in to avoid danger from the fumes.

There are dozens of commercial products available that have made furniture refinishing easier than ever before. One product can simply be brushed on a piece of furniture, left standing for a few hours and wiped off, taking all the old paint with it. If you have a shop or garage connected to your home which you can transform into a furniture refinishing room, you have all the space you need to carry on your business.

Prices for refinishing furniture depend, of course, on the piece of furniture itself, how many layers of paint have been applied to it, how decorative the furniture is and how much detail work is required to refinish it. You should figure your costs on the basis of $5 an hour. If you are not paying rent for a shop, you should be able to clear at least $4.50 of this $5 as profit.

This is a business in which elbow grease is the largest investment and materials the smallest. Advertise your service in the Yellow Pages and in classified ads. Also have a moderate quantity of business cards printed which you should leave with prospective customers. Visit used furniture stores (they may want to refer customers to you). You will be servicing both the furniture store and the furniture buyer at the same time. If your customers want special work done, such as furniture restoration or reupholstery, your charges will be extra.

It is not difficult to reupholster a cushion; but it is quite difficult to reupholster a complete piece of furniture. You should limit your reupholstery, at least at the beginning, to simple cushions. You will charge your customers extra for materials in this case, though you can invite them to provide their own material for reupholstering.

As your business increases in size, consider renting a larger work area. You do not need a location like that required by a retail store. You might even consider using someone else's abandoned garage.

You should have a station wagon to transport furniture to your workshop; if the piece of furniture is too large for a station wagon, a U-Haul trailer or a small truck. In this case you will charge your customer for pickup and delivery.

Most people willingly pay well to have their furniture refinished because no matter how much the cost, it is a mere fraction of what it would cost to replace the furniture. If you become well known for quality work, you might be asked to refinish valuable antiques, at which time your workmanship will command a higher rate of pay.

You will have to use your discretion as you get further into this business. If possible, start with furniture that is not of great antique value, until you have perfected your skills. Of course, one of the best ways to acquire these skills is to work with a furniture refinisher as an employee. As we have repeated so often, there is no better way to learn than to do.

15 · We-Drive-Your-Car Service

There are many reasons why people want a professional driver to drive their cars. Vacationers going on long trips, where they expect to be away for several months at a time, frequently want to arrive at their destination quickly by airplane. Yet they would love to have the use of their own car once they get there. A perfect solution is to pay someone to drive the car for them. It is usually cheaper than shipping a car and certainly costs less than renting a car for an extended period of time.

There are other reasons too. Assume you and your family are going to an airport fifty miles away. It could cost you $50 or more in limousine fees if one were available from an airport limousine service. But call a We-Drive-Your-Car Service and for about $10 a "professional" driver will take you and your whole family to the airport in your car using your gas. The driver will then return your car to your house, lock it and put the key where you want it left. The result is that you have transported your whole family in your own auto for one-fifth of what it would have cost for a limousine service, and you had the convenience of leaving when you wanted. Another advantage: Suppose your uncle and his whole family were coming to visit you by train and you couldn't pick them up; you could hire the service to pick up your uncle's family and bring them back to your house at far less than it would have cost you to pay for a taxi.

To start a We-Drive-Your Car Service requires very little investment. The first thing you should do is compile a list of drivers whom you can call on quick notice for either short or long trips. One good source of help is a local college where students are frequently looking for part-time work that does not require regular hours. Place a classified ad and ask for: "Part-time help, driver's license required. Men and women welcome. Flexible hours." Put together a list of as many as twenty or thirty drivers, noting next to the name and telephone number of each what hours they are available to work.

Make an additional list of drivers who are available for long trips, say from New York to Florida. In exchange for getting there for free, they will drive your client's car.

Check with your automobile insurance agent to find out how much "floater" policies cost, so that your drivers are covered in different cars. Advertise the fact that you are bonded, if indeed you can get bonding at a reasonable price. This will obviously reassure your clients. Take a listing in the Yellow Pages under "Auto Transportation" or "Driving Services."

When figuring your prices to clients, bear in mind that your price does not include gas and oil. Customers will be expected to pay for fuel in addition to the auto transport charge. You should charge 5¢ to 7¢ a mile for long trips. For shorter trips to deliver families fifty miles away or so, you should charge 10¢ a mile. For very short trips in town, for pickups and deliveries in which people want you to use their car, you should have a minimum flat fee of, say, $10, assuming that it does not take more than one hour to complete the pickup or delivery.

You should be able to pay a salary to your drivers of no more than $2.50 an hour. Also, make it understood that they are expected to get to the point of departure, that is your client's house, by their own means. If one of your drivers doesn't have a car, make it understood that he will have to use public transportation. Adjust this policy depending on how easy it is to get from one place to the other by public transportation in your area.

Possibilities for growth in this business are substantial—and are limited only by the number of drivers available and the number of people who want their cars driven. What this means is that you could conceivably have a "staff" of as many as thirty or forty people working for you at the same time.

16 · Art Sales

There is something about owning an original piece of art that thrills many people. Unfortunately, many good, original paintings are beyond the means of most people. There is an exception, of course: the mass-produced "paintings" which are done on an assembly line overseas. But for those who prefer paintings that take longer than fifteen minutes to produce, there is really very little selection under $100.

You can fill a need for good, less expensive original art without resorting to the mass-produced works. This less expensive art is in the form of original etchings, lithographs, woodcuts, sketches and even some paintings.

There are virtually thousands of young artists throughout the country, many of them studying right in your own area in art schools and colleges, who produce sizable quantities of very attractive artwork that sells for under $100.

An advertisement in your local paper expressing a desire to represent various artists with works selling for less than $100 will bring you a slew of inquiries faster than you thought possible. If there is one thing every artist wants it's to sell his work. And there are a great many more artists than there are people in a position to sell art. You can put together a thriving business based on this less expensive art, once you have acquired a "stable" of promising young artists.

To begin an art sales business do not spend money renting display space. The first thing you should do is set up a room in your home in which you can show artwork; use drawers or shelves to hold additional artwork. In this way you can create a "gallery" in one part of your home (without making it look like a retail store).

Run classified ads offering original art at prices under $100. Stress that this is not imported art but works of artists residing in the area. You will get some inquiries directly at your home, but don't count on this way of doing business to bring you all your art sales. In addition, go to various furniture stores. Explain the kind of artwork you have for sale and the number of different artists you represent. Furniture stores frequently like to refer their customers to others who can provide accessories that the furniture store itself may not carry. You should also try to arrange for art showings at local "Y"s, church meeting rooms and local schools and colleges.

Interior decorators are another good outlet for sales. Make it your business to contact as many local decorators as possible, and leave your business cards with them. Decorators are frequently looking for ways to add unique, tasteful touches to the work they do for their clients. Original art, especially art that sells at reasonable prices, is a very attractive way to give someone's home a touch of uniqueness and individuality.

Have your artists sign a contract which gives you an exclusive right to sell their work, at least for a distinct period of time. When you sell a piece of art, the usual commission is from one-third to one-half of the selling price.

You can earn additional income from your art sales by associating with a local frame shop, or even hiring someone who is a good framer. You should take the framing cost and add one-third to arrive at the cost you should charge your customer.

If you build up a good stable of artists and you can align yourself with people like interior decorators and furniture store owners, as well as sell to the public, you are likely to have a steady stream of satisfied clients which could grow quickly in a reasonably short time. At that point you can consider renting store space for yourself. However, keep your out-of-pocket investment of cash to a minimum, at least at the beginning.

17 · Resumes

Chances for success in this home business are greater when there is a high rate of unemployment. As more people are out of work, and therefore looking for jobs, there will be a greater need for your service. Providing a résumé service means you take a person's work background and put it into a readable format so that this person can present a clear, quick picture of his occupational history. If you don't live in a large city, consider advertising in the nearest large city, because that is where most of your clients will come from. You will be dealing for the most part with office workers and teachers, college professors and the like (at college level a résumé is called a curriculum vitae).

The basic tools to begin this business are a typewriter and a knowledge of grammar, spelling and punctuation. It is helpful if you have a facility for writing, since part of your service will depend on your ability to improve on résumés if necessary. You might also be asked to construct the whole résumé from just an interview with a client. Strange as it sounds, many people have never had to put together a résumé because they have had the same job for so many years.

You can consult business textbooks to find out how to construct a résumé. Better still, if you have not put together résumés before, contact a friend or acquaintance who works in the personnel office of a large firm. Ask him or her what personnel officers look for in a résumé. There is not just one way to organize someone's work history. It depends a great deal on the industry in which that person works. A point to remember when you are interviewing a client is that you want to get as much pertinent material about the person's work background in as short a space as possible. Bear in mind, too, that personnel officers for various companies, especially in bad times, are literally deluged with résumés from thousands of applicants, many for the same job.

Your service can become truly invaluable if you are able to put together a résumé that will get your client positive attention. After all, the purpose of the résumé is to get your client's prospective employer to grant an interview.

Begin promoting your service with a classified ad in the largest nearby city (if you are not already living there). Give your telephone number and stress that *your résumés get results.* Meet with your clients personally, especially if they have never had a résumé prepared before. Develop techniques to elicit important information from your client. Your résumé service is in many ways a job consultation service. Once you have acquired the pertinent facts from your client, type up the résumé neatly and succinctly. When it is appropriate, suggest two or three separate résumés for the same client. This will happen if your client is applying for several different kinds of jobs. Each résumé should be directed toward one job only and should not try to encompass half a dozen different kinds of work experience. Remember, people who hire job applicants are looking for those who come closest to fulfilling their ideal for the job. For instance, if a woman is looking for a job as a legal secretary and part of her work background includes preparing contracts for a real estate office, stress the contract preparation part of her job. On the other hand, if she is applying for a job as purchasing agent for a building contractor, stress the fact that she has spent a great amount of time working in a real estate office and has had experience with property dealers. The point is that the résumé should emphasize those aspects of the job for which your client is applying. The less extraneous material in the résumé, the easier it is for a prospective employer to appreciate the qualifications of your client.

After preparing one or more résumés for your client, you are responsible for duplicating the résumés in whatever quantity is necessary. You can either rent a mimeograph machine or deal with an offset printer. An offset printer will charge somewhere in the neighborhood of $4 per 100 copies printed. All you need supply to the printer is a cleanly typed sheet of white paper. In some cases a photograph may be helpful as part of your client's résumé. If this is the case, an offset printer is your only option. Besides, printing usually looks more professional than mimeographing.

When you figure your fee, be flexible. If all you've had to do is type a résumé and put the person's work qualifications in order, you should charge approximately $10 for 100 copies. Assuming it takes you no longer than a half hour to type up the material you've been given, you earn a $6 gross profit on 100 copies. If, on the other hand, you are acting as a job consultant, charge your client by the hour. Allow between $5 and $10 an hour for your time, plus costs for reproducing the résumés.

Obviously, as your résumé service becomes more in demand, you should enjoy a growing awareness of job markets and how to reach them. You could easily be in a position to branch out as an employment consultation service. Your fee, by the hour, could jump to $10, $15, even $20 or more, depending on the sophistication of the job for which your clients are applying.

18 · Interior Decorating Service

There was a time when only the rich could afford to have a consultant come in and advise them on how to decorate a room. These exclusive interior decorators dealt with the most expensive furniture stores and accessory shops. But now more and more people are realizing the benefits of having a professional guide them in putting together colors, styles of furniture, tasteful accessories, and other components that will give their rooms not only a beautiful appearance but a very personal touch.

Far from being an exclusive domain of the rich, interior decorating consultation is now a service that can help middle income people achieve attractive unified room settings, as well as *save them money*. How does a decorator save money? Interior decorators make it their business to know where to shop, how much things cost, and how to cut back on expenses when necessary. They also become specialists in finding bargains. A good decorator knows lots of tricks to furnish on a low budget, as well as where accessories can be purchased that are both tasteful and inexpensive.

An interior decorator's fee can be based either on a consultation rate per hour (usually $10) or on a percentage (10 percent to 15 percent) of the total amount of money the client will spend on interior decoration.

Announce your service through a listing in the Yellow Pages and a classified ad. As your business grows, you will discover that more and more clients come to you through word-of-mouth recommendations. Emphasize in your presentations that your service could end up costing less than if the client bought furniture and accessories by herself.

Have business cards printed. Use your home address and telephone number since this is a business in which you visit the client much more frequently than vice versa.

You must also become closely associated with retailers in your area who will not only offer a large selection of furniture and accessories to choose from, but will give you an interior decorator's discount (15 percent or more). You must also familiarize yourself with unusual places to buy, such as secondhand shops, antique stores, even thrift shops. You might be surprised to see how many bargains lie hidden in the corners, mostly in used-goods stores. You should also get to know a local furniture refinisher who can take a prized, inexpensive piece and turn it into an exquisite-looking "antique" at less than it would have cost your client to buy a finished piece.

There are many ways to educate yourself in the subtleties of interior decoration. Textbooks on color matching and coordination of styles are some of your best sources for decorating ideas. Magazines like *Better Homes and Gardens* and *Interior Decorating Annual* contain full-color pictures of literally hundreds of room settings. You will discover that you can take one idea from one room setting, several ideas from another and put together a unique concept that will appeal to your client for its beauty and individuality.

With a supply of graph paper you can become adept at designing floor plans, an absolute necessity for your trade. When you see clients, solicit ideas, ask them if they have seen pictures in a magazine that illustrate features they would like to see in their homes.

The most important task in interior decorating is to draw from your client what effect he or she wants to create, and then show them how to execute that effect. You should also get to know about the contracting services available in your community. If part of an interior decorating consultation involves construction, you should be able to suggest carpenters for the job. When you calculate your fee, keep in mind that if you have put together a complete home package for a client you are entitled to a fee for *all* of your time, including the time you spend on the job as renovation is taking place. This is why many decorators charge a percentage of the total cost for the job, because it becomes difficult to gauge how much time will be necessary to spend supervising and consulting. If your consultation is limited to suggestions for floor plans, furniture and accessories, then you are in a better position to charge by the hour. This is a business in which your expertise should improve quickly. As you take on each job it will be a new and exciting experience in which you will not only impart valuable information to your client but will be gaining experience for yourself.

Since part of your service may include sending clients to furniture stores and accessory shops, arrange in advance for the store owner to give your client the decorator's discount. A business card presented to a local merchant will usually suffice to establish your credentials as a legitimate decorator. Of course, the more frequently you patronize a merchant, the better the relationship.

The basic ingredients of a successful interior decorator are: an artistic flair, flexibility, a knack for understanding your client's needs, and an imaginative way to execute your client's desires at a cost determined in advance. After you have completed one or more consultations, take photographs of your work. This can be done with inexpensive color snapshots. The point is to create a portfolio that will offer evidence of your success when soliciting other clients. You will have no difficulty getting permission to photograph clients' rooms since most people are proud of a room that has been freshly decorated to their tastes.

Your expenses should be limited to the advertising mentioned above and a generous number of subscriptions to leading interior decorating magazines, as well as the consumer magazines devoted to beautifying homes. You may also find it interesting to note that *Forbes* magazine called interior decorating "perhaps the hottest growth field of the 1970s."

19 · Sandwich Wagon

One of the disadvantages for people working in an industrial area is the extreme difficulty in getting good food to eat nearby. Most manufacturing districts cannot support full-time restaurants. To provide fresh lunches for these and other workers you can create your own sandwich wagon. You can use a station wagon, or even a car. It is not necessary to invest any money in a van or truck of any sort.

Your first step is to write a menu of sandwiches you want to make. Keep it simple but good. You don't have to buy expensive wraps for your sandwiches, wax paper will do. Be sure that all the supplies you carry to serve your customers are paper—paper cups, paper plates and paper wrappers. In addition to sandwiches include a selection of soft drinks, prepackaged if possible, and a coffee urn. Also include an array of desserts, preferably single-wrapped pastries.

In addition to industrial sites, prime selling areas are public parks, open-air concerts, playground areas, even local college campuses. Your menu will have to vary depending upon what is availble in the area you are working, as well as the desires of your customers. This knowledge will come quickly with experience.

One of the advantages of this business is that you recover your investment for food almost the same day you lay out your cash. Figure your pricing on this basis: If it costs you 20¢ to make a sandwich, you should charge customers at least 40¢. There is an exception to this double-your-cost rule. If sandwiches of the same type sell in your area for 60¢ instead of 40¢, adjust your pricing so that it is competitive, yet still allows you a higher profit. If an item that you sell costs you more than half of your selling price, stop making it. (You are not in the business of providing food at a loss.) The 50 percent minimum profit you realize on each piece of food you sell will take care of your expenses for driving from one place to the other as well as give you money for your time.

One way to increase your business is to solicit local establishments that do not serve food, such as bars. Offer to supply ready-made sandwiches on a wholesale basis. In this case, you need not get double your cost for the food. Rather, you must leave room for the retailer to make a profit. Since you are selling in bulk quantities you can afford to take a mark-up of one-third above your costs.

You could also consider soliciting local vending machine operators. Suggest to them that you will prepare food on a wholesale basis for placement in their vending machines.

All of these additional services can put you in business as a prepared-food wholesaler. You may find that this business could outgrow your sandwich wagon very quickly. But the place to start, because there is no appreciable investment, is in selling retail from the back of your own vehicle.

20 · Antique Dealer

This is a highly specialized but fascinating business. Your success depends in great part on your ability to acquire valuable goods, preferably of antique value, at low prices and resell them for a substantial profit. It's extremely enjoyable if you enjoy browsing through secondhand shops, estate sales, attics, tag sales and auctions. Look hard enough and you can come upon property that is of hidden antique value. This happens frequently at estate auctions where the entire contents of a home are being sold at one time. Many dealers have discovered first-edition books, furniture that looks useless yet may be of genuine antique value, as well as valuable dishes and dinnerware.

You might have to purchase a dozen books to find one that is a legitimate first edition, but if you do find one it is well worth the effort. If you are not already an antique buff you must educate yourself to the values of antiques. There is a reference book available at most libraries that is updated annually and gives going prices for goods of certain periods. You won't come across great bargains every day, but if you specialize in a particular type of antique, such as furniture or tapestries or china or rare books, you can soon become an expert in this field.

You do not need an office or retail shop to carry on your business. It is advisable to have a space in your home, preferably a garage or basement room, where you can safely store articles.

To learn what sells, spend afternoons visiting antique shops and secondhand stores. Talk to the owners, if possible, and find out what kinds of things move best. You may be surprised to find that an old kerosene lamp, or an old carpet, tarnished candlesticks, a broken rocking chair—all or any of these items—may be an invaluable antique underneath the dust.

To sell your items, advertise directly in the classified section of the newspaper. List specifically the kinds of things you have for sale. Antique dealers could be among your most valued customers. They know bargains when they see them, and even if they have to pay more for the item than you did, they know someone else may want a particular article and will be willing to pay for it.

Consider holding a garage sale at your home when you have acquired enough goods to pique the public's interest. You do not have to spend any additional cash except for your classified advertisement. Once your business grows, you may find it desirable to set up a retail store. In addition, solicit interior decorators and announce that you are constantly acquiring different kinds of goods that might interest their clients.

Your potential profit in this field is really without limit. You can find items for as little as 10¢, 25¢, on up to hundreds of dollars, that you can resell for five and ten times or more than what you paid. People do not expect antiques to be priced as one would price conventional retail goods. An antique by definition is something rare, and people expect to pay high sums for antiques of genuine value.

If you are not sure of the value of certain articles you acquire, there are professional appraisers who can date items and confirm their actual value.

Appraisers charge a fee based on the value of the item, but their appraisals are considered gospel. Insurance companies use these official appraisals when they are determining the value of special property. Therefore you can be certain that an appraisal by a professional is the legitimate "value" of the article you own.

21 · Messenger-Delivery Service

In almost every business you can think of, whether it is retailing, manufacturing or a service business, there is a need for quick, direct delivery of envelopes and small packages. In many cases this need cannot be left to the post office, either because it takes too long or the item must be delivered by hand. In large cities particularly, delivery-messenger services do a very brisk business.

To start this specialized service you need no investment except your own car. Or you could even use a motorcycle or bicycle. This is a business that can be started out of your own home with just a telephone (or you can hire an answering service). Since you are likely to be handling irreplaceable messages and packages, your service should be bonded. This can be done for little money and will more than pay for itself in the added reliability you offer your customers.

Begin by running ads in your local newspaper. The key features of this service are speed and reliability. Stress that immediate delivery is available, as well as regular pickup and delivery service. If you live in an outlying suburb (where more and more businesses are beginning to locate), you have a ready market for those industries that must communicate regularly with a nearby city. Once your business is established, you can hire a staff of messengers who, if they do not have their own vehicles, can use public transportation.

In addition to advertising in the local paper, it would be well worth your while to have business cards and a few hundred brochures which you can send to a list of companies that you draw right from the Yellow Pages of your community's telephone book. Your most likely prospects will probably be advertising agencies, financial services and others who have a constant need for quick delivery and pickup of small items. Advertising agencies in particular depend on messenger services to get their materials to publications before deadlines. After you have mailed a number of brochures, follow up with telephone calls to these companies. Ask for personal interviews so that you can sell your service in person.

The fees you charge will be based on several kinds of service. You can have a one-time charge for special deliveries. To arrive at that figure you must calculate your expenses for either gasoline or public transportation, a salary to your messengers, if you have a staff, and your expenses for insurance and bonding. Take these raw costs and double them.

When a company has an important message or package to be delivered, they expect to pay substantially more than postal rates for this service. If you have organized your schedule well, you should be able to make regular runs and still give each customer the individualized service he expects. Therefore, if it costs $5 for a round-trip train ticket, and it will take approximately three hours for the message or package to be delivered, you can charge as much as $20 to $30 for a specially delivered item. If you combine the pickups and deliveries well, so that you can deliver several items at the same time, you can charge less and make your rates even more competitive.

The goal of your business is to make it as efficient as possible. Therefore, if you can offer your customers a regular schedule at one rate and a special-delivery service at a higher rate, you are putting together an attractive, flexible package.

You can get a staff by advertising for part-time help in the local newspaper. Scheduling can be arranged to suit your employees' needs, since you can arrange to have different staff members make trips at certain times of the day.

Try to arrange to have at least one messenger available at all times, including yourself if necessary. The more reliable and available your service, the more successful it will become.

The growth potential of your business is sizable. You can increase and decrease the size of your staff easily, especially since no training is required for this job. When considering part-time workers for staff assignments, make sure that they are conscientious and dependable. One serious mishap can put a permanent dent in your business, especially if your customer is a regular.

When setting your rates, try first to get customers to sign up for a regular contract. That is, a certain number of deliveries each week or each month at the same time. You will be billing customers on a monthly basis, except for those accounts which you only serve once in a while (or for the first time), in which case you should ask for payment of the bill upon proof of delivery.

You should have a supply of receipts which can be printed with your name. Receipts are also available in blank form at a lower price. You must be sure that every package that goes out is signed for at both ends. Your receipts will be the only proof that you have performed your service.

To figure rates for frequently traveled routes, run the message or package yourself, at least the first time. There is no better way to convince yourself of how long it takes to perform a service.

And bear in mind that the messengers you hire to work for you will be representing you in every way. If their attitudes suit your customers, it will reflect on you and your business. If there is a question of reliability, it is better to reject a prospective employee than take the risk that he will harm your business. This kind of business will be very appealing to people looking for part-time work, and you should have no trouble filling a staff as quickly as you need it.

22 · Booking Agents

Here is a business that is both exciting and rewarding and can be run from your home with no outlay of cash, except for small advertisements. To put together your own booking agency first requires that you have a broad selection of talented, professional entertainers available to you exclusively, at least in your area. You can start with just one versatile group of entertainers, such as a popular dance band.

You can discover talent just as everyone else does—by going to nightclubs, concerts, coffee houses, even large parties. Most entertainers are anxious to register with as many booking agents as possible, since this obviously increases their chances of getting work. Once you have acquired the exclusive booking rights to an act in an area, you have the nucleus for your booking agency.

The next step is to run small ads in the newspaper offering "Entertainment for All Occasions." Your ad, and a listing in the Yellow Pages, will bring you inquiries sooner or later. However, don't rely only on these advertisements to get your business going quickly. Contact personally the entertainment chairmen of local organizations. Church groups, "Y" groups, even local college and school organizations frequently plan entertainment bills around live music. Whether it's for fund-raising or a football homecoming weekend, or even a senior prom, organizations are always looking for talented groups to entertain.

Even if the evening of entertainment is several months off, you will do well to organize your solicitations early. Most large events are planned far in advance. Sell the entertainment chairman on the experience and excitement of the group or entertainer you represent. Stress how you can also help in advertising for the event by providing glossy photos of the entertainers along with promotional advice.

Your fee as a booking agent is usually 10 percent of the entertainers' fee. If a band is making $250 for one night's work at a large dance, your share is $25. Once your stable of entertainers grows, you could have five, ten or twelve groups working at the same time. Your fees for one week could easily amount to $250 or more.

Of course, the best way to keep your entertainer-clients happy is to get them as much work as possible. Be selective when considering taking on an entertainer. Unfortunately, there are hundreds more entertainers trying to break into show business than there are booking agents able to handle them. Most of your business time will probably be spent getting jobs for your entertainers.

In this business your energy and your eye for talent will be the deciding factors in your success. Although you will learn by doing, you cannot really train for this job. It is just something that you either have a feel for or you don't. Basically you must have an instinct for what people want in entertainment. Some of the situations are obvious. If you're dealing with a college group who wants a rock-style band to entertain, you won't succeed by talking them into hiring a 1950s dance band.

When you book entertainers, at least at the beginning, plan on spending time checking them wherever they are working. Get a good feel for how they work with an audience. Try not to rely simply on an entertainer's credits to convince you that he or she is worth handling. Go see for yourself.

The potential in this business is enormous. If you develop a good record of getting work for your entertainers, they in turn will recommend you to other new top talent. Don't be afraid to make mistakes. It happens. And don't let the entertainers crowd your telephone with inquiries about work. Make sure they understand "Don't call us, we'll call you."

23 · Custom Greeting Cards

Although the greeting card business is seasonal to some extent (Christmas is still the number one season), there is a growing need for custom cards of all types. You don't have to have an artistic flair necessarily, although it certainly helps. Your custom greeting cards can take the form of either designs you manufacture yourself or photographs supplied by individual customers.

Again, this is a business that can be run from your home without much overhead. The first step is to make several kinds of unique greeting cards. You can cut designs in linoleum blocks with cutting tools that are readily available and easy to use. Then you ink the block and roll it onto blank heavy stock paper you can pick up at any stationery store. In essence, you are putting together your own catalog of greeting cards. This is not as difficult as it might seem. All you need is ten to twenty different kinds of cards to start your "portfolio." Once you have put together this group of cards, place a sample of each in a notebook with acetate sheets to protect the cards. You can design cards that feature a family photograph or an individual photo, or you can reproduce illustrations from magazines that you paste on the front of the card.

Advertise your custom greeting cards in small classified ads in the local newspaper. This is for starters only. In addition to direct sales to individuals, you can take your portfolio to other greeting card stores, drugstores, children's stores and boutiques.

The greeting cards need not only be those designed for a special occasion, like Christmas or a birthday. You can prepare cards that say nothing inside, and in fact become useful as informal notes. This is one way to turn a seasonal business into a business that is good for any time of the year. Custom cards do not have to sell on a standard 50 percent mark-up from wholesale to retail. If the cards are artistically designed and very individual, such as the type made by applying unique illustrations, you can sometimes get three, four and five times your costs. Get friends to give you old issues of popular magazines. You can frequently find dozens of full-color illustrations that will fit perfectly as card decorations. In this way you're actually creating a set of cards which are unique and cannot be duplicated.

Offer the stores you visit the right to hold a box of your cards on consignment. That is, they pay you after they sell them. You can afford to do this in most cases because your investment is really quite small. A box of twelve cards, for instance, could cost you as little as 25¢ or 50¢ in materials. These cards, by the box, might sell for as much as $4 or $5. Once you have been able to place sample cards in various stores, you will be in a good position to take custom orders for cards.

Offer to have personal photographs printed on greeting cards. The mechanics are quite simple: Take a photograph (black-and-white photos will cost much less than color) and bring your high-quality paper stock to any offset printer. He can manufacture a small quantity for you. One hundred printed cards may cost you as much as $4 or $6 to manufacture, but can be sold for $10 or more.

Make your business as versatile as possible. For instance, show blank note cards in which you could then print greetings for Christmas, Valentine's Day, Easter, birthdays, or anniversaries. You can offer to hand-sign the names of the people sending the cards. This could be popular at Christmastime when families send a large number of cards and wish to avoid the impersonal look of preprinted names.

Additional markets for your custom designs are the large card manufacturers themselves. If, for instance, you have designed a lovely linoleum cut for Valentine's Day, submit a sample of the card to a manufacturer like Hallmark or Gibson. If one of these companies buys your card, they will pay you a fee that could amount to as much as $50, $100, or more for the right to print your design.

Stationery stores and bookshops are particularly good markets for cards that you want to sell on consignment. A local bookshop will probably be willing to display your cards because they don't take much space and the store owner knows you will be able to fill orders quickly.

Make it your business to include custom notes which people can use at all times of the year. If you have affluent customers, offer to design a card that will be specifically representative of them, whether it's a design incorporating their name or even something that they own, such as a boat. Once you have begun your business you might find it worthwhile to prepare a brochure that reproduces several of your card designs.

The custom greeting card business has a high profit potential, especially because custom greeting cards by definition cannot be manufactured on a large scale. Individual craftsmen like you are the sole source of supply. Just make sure that when you price your cards, whether it's for wholesale or retail distribution, you take into account not only your cost for materials, but the full time necessary to produce the cards, including trips to the printer.

24 · Consignment Shop

Most people have literally crates of used items around their homes like clothing, dishes, unmatched silverware, children's toys, even small appliances that they no longer have a need for. If people were reminded that they could receive money for these items, they would probably waste little time in collecting them.

You can start a business in which you sell used items, without paying out a cent until you've made the sale. What we are talking about is a consignment shop. "Consignment" means people give you merchandise and get paid only if and when you sell the merchandise. This is the best way for you to obtain a substantial inventory of retail goods without risking any money to pay for them.

A basic prerequisite for a consignment shop is that you have a place to display the goods. Your "store" need by nothing more than a large room in a commercial district of your town, in which you need spend very little for decorations and accessories. In fact a shop that is simply filled with lots of shelves and racks is suitable. You needn't even be concerned with repainting.

You invite people to bring goods to your consignment shop by means of a classified ad. Ask for items by particular names such as: clothing in good condition, toys that are not broken, dishes and glassware that do not have too many chips, as well as general knick-knacks and other small items that people have grown tired of or no longer have any use for, but may be useful to others.

When people bring goods to your shop, you must tell them immediately how much you are willing to pay for the item when it is sold. Make sure these people understand that they will get paid only after you have sold the item. You might set a policy of holding an item for consignment for a limited amount of time, say two months. If the item has not been sold by that time, you have the option of returning it to its original owner (and the owner has the option of claiming it back).

If you can keep your store rent to less than $100 a month, you have a minimum risk of investment. Your customers will be drawn by the bargain nature of what you have to offer. You will be able to sell whole sets of dishes, for instance, for less than $10 (and you probably will have to pay no more than $2 to the original owner when it is sold). If you solicit for used clothing, make it clear that you expect the clothing to be cleaned before giving it to the shop. Scrutinize the goods that come in. Make sure the items you accept are in reasonably good condition because you will not be able to afford the time or the money to recondition the goods. They will have to be sold as is.

When advertising for customers, stress that goods will be sold for up to 90 percent off their original prices. Few bargain hunters can resist the lure of finding a useful and valuable piece of merchandise at such extraordinary savings.

If you have the space in your store, you can take in larger appliances, such as used TV sets in running order or even washing machines and dryers. A lack of merchandise will not be a problem. Most people throw away perfectly good items simply because no one has brought the value of their goods to their attention.

Prepare a large hand-lettered sign for your shop window. The object of your store is to create the impression of low overhead (which indeed it is). This business, in fact, is probably the least expensive retail business one could start.

Try to display your items neatly with different types of merchandise in strategic locations around the store, but do not be concerned with large display space. Use one series of shelves for dishes and pile them on top of each other. Just make sure people can look at the goods without breaking them. You can even use corrugated boxes to hold clothing and inexpensive pipe racks to hold items like coats, suits and dresses that can be hung on hangers. Your consignment shop should have a look of pleasant clutter.

Unlike a more formal retail establishment you do not have to have a large staff that goes around refolding clothes and restacking merchandise. Your customers should feel free to browse through boxes and shelves without the feeling that they are "messing up" your shop. You should be able to man the shop by yourself and you need only stay open during regular business hours.

If rent on a low-overhead outlet is beyond your means right now, you could even start your consignment shop in your garage. Your classified ads would invite people to visit your "shop" in the same way that tag sales and garage sales entice customers to people's homes. Aside from advertising and your modest rent if you have a retail location, you need only invest in a few other items like receipts and sales slips. You do not have to have a cash register. In fact a cigar box would reinforce your low-overhead image. You must give everyone who brings in merchandise for consignment a receipt for their goods. On it you state the price you will pay them if the goods are sold and the time you wish to hold the goods. You must also, of course, give receipts to your customers. Your policy on returns will have to be dictated by the item you are selling. Most customers at consignment shops expect to buy merchandise as is.

Consignment shops were originally started to raise money for charities. But it wasn't long before people with personal profit in mind discovered them. If your shop is successful, you will find it quite easy to branch out. Your low overhead dictates that you look for any large room in a commercial district which can accommodate ten or fifteen customers, as well as a sizable inventory of merchandise. Some consignment shops specialize only in clothing, or furniture, or toys and small appliances. Your chances for success in the beginning will be greater if you have a wide selection of merchandise.

With the success of your business, you can think of expanding to include pickups with either a station wagon or small van. In this way you will be able to acquire more valuable merchandise by offering to actually go to the owner's home and cart it away for him.

25 · Private Tour Guide

The basic job of a tour guide is to take individuals or groups on trips and to make sure that all their needs are looked after. (This is the most general definition.) You can lead a tour to Europe, to vacation spots in this country, or your tour can mean taking youngsters on a camping trip overnight. The possibilities in this field are vast. You probably won't be in a position to offer tours of every type but choose the specialty that appeals to you most.

If you like the outdoors and have been a camper yourself, you can consider yourself qualified to lead youngsters on overnight trips or even longer camping trips to virtually any part of the country. Of course, it will pay for you to have been to the area before. Make sure the campsite is in an area in which *you* have traveled. If it's within driving distance from your home, visit the campsite before you actually escort a group of youngsters there.

If you are a seasoned traveler, either in Europe or this country, you can set up tours for limited groups in which you not only act as a sightseeing guide but as an official who makes sure facilities are running smoothly. Whatever your choice of tour, the methods for setting up your guide service are similar.

The first step, before you even take out your first tour, is to associate yourself with a local travel agency (this is assuming you wish to guide the more conventional tours that adult vacationers enjoy taking). Explain to a travel agent what you have in mind. The basic trip will be put together through the commercial agency, and you, in addition to a free trip, will get a fee for guiding this tour.

Let's say, for instance, you want to lead a tour of eight to fifteen adults to one of our more famous national parks, like Grand Canyon or Yosemite. The first thing you would do is set up accommodations through a travel agency. Find out exactly how much this group-cost will be, then work through with the travel agent exactly how much the trip will cost as a package per individual.

The travel agent in this case is acting as your personal agent. He or she should actually make the reservations for transportation and hotels, using the travel agency's facilities for instant confirmation.

Your job will be to promote the tour and acquire customers for your group.

Your fee should be based on one flat rate for the whole trip. Let's say the travel agent gives you the group rate for transportation, hotels and any other features of the trip such as sightseeing buses, etc. You then add to this group fee your own fee. If you will be away for one week your fee should be the equivalent of a week's pay (somewhere between $150 and $250). With bargain group rates available, as they are with airplanes, you should be able to present a package to your customers that will cost them little, if anything, more than a trip they arranged themselves.

Arranging camping trips for youngsters can be done more easily by yourself. Select a camping or canoeing area that is not too far to drive in half a day. Again, be sure you have scouted this area thoroughly yourself. When escorting youngsters on a trip you should be particularly aware of your needs for insurance. Contact your local agent for details. The insurance for a trip of one week's duration or less will not be prohibitive and will be well worth the protection. You do not need a license to escort people on tours (but your competence will show very quickly regardless).

What your rates are for a conventional tour will depend to a great extent on the package cost from your travel agent. It is easier to figure how much you can make on something like a camping trip which you organize and lead yourself.

Once you have decided to organize a trip for fifteen teen-agers (it is probably wise to include only youngsters over the age of twelve) you should charge $5 to $8 per day, per youngster. This charge will be in addition to bus fare, if necessary. Fifteen youngsters at, say, $7 a day gives you a gross revenue of $105 per day. You should be able to net over $50 as your fee, taking into account the cost of food and supplies. For a seven-day trip this can bring you in excess of $350 for a week's work.

You need not limit your tour guiding to long trips. You can also organize interesting day trips for youngsters or adults, either after school, on Saturdays, even during holiday vacations. For a fee of $5 per child you could take ten youngsters to an amusement park for an afternoon and realize a profit of $25 or more for just a few hours' work. This is a particularly attractive service for parents who want to throw birthday celebrations for their children, but who cannot manage a whole group by themselves. You can also organize trips to museums, beaches, famous historical sites, zoos, even the movies and ball games.

As your business grows, you can begin to hire a staff of adults (preferably no one younger than college age). In this way you could end up becoming the administrator of this business and realize a handsome profit without actually going on the tours yourself.

Keep in mind that expenses for any kind of tour should be based on costs for accommodations, plus a fee for your time.

Advertise your service in the classified section of your local newspaper. If your business grows quickly enough, you can also advertise in the travel section of larger city newspapers. Choose your tour-guide specialty with an eye toward what kind of trips you enjoy most. Although this can be a lucrative business it should obviously appeal to you personally.

In addition to print advertising you can contact local groups with a brochure offering your service. Be sure to make all of your arrangements in advance and allow plenty of time for reservations. Ask your customers for a deposit (approximately one-third of the package cost of the tour) to confirm their reservations. This will protect you in the event that individuals cannot make the trip for one reason or another.

You can begin and even run this business right from your own home. If you will be doing most of the organizing and tour guiding yourself, it will pay to have an answering service available to act as your "receptionist." '

26 · Specialty Food Selling

Most home cooks have a specialty dish that they are particularly adept at preparing, whether it's a delectable rice pilaff, chicken pie or fresh pickled cucumbers. You probably have a favorite yourself that draws great compliments when you serve it at home. Whatever your food specialty, you can create a market for it right in your own community.

One woman had a delicacy that her friends loved. She made three or four different kinds of relish in her own kitchen, corn relish, pickled relish and other types that were a delicious seasoning for a number of foods. She had been making these preserves only at Christmas and using them as gifts. When someone suggested she sell these relishes to local gourmet shops, she was surprised. She never thought there would be a market outside her home for these delicious seasonings. But there was, and she found that by offering two or three types of relish in a local gourmet shop, the demand for her product grew very quickly.

She was able to put up a small mason jar of relish for less than 50¢. Because of the unique recipe, and the fact that these relishes were so unusual and delicious, she was able to sell each jar for $1.25 to the gourmet shop which in turn sold it to retail customers for $2.

If you have a specialty that you enjoy cooking, you can put together several samples, then visit shops in your area. You can also solicit customers directly through classified advertising and small posters placed in strategic locations. If you advertise directly *and* sell to retail stores, keep in mind that your pricing to direct customers should not compete unfavorably with the retail price your goods are being offered for in stores.

The investment for your specialty-food selling business, in addition to an advertising budget, should include a generous supply of labels as well as containers for your goods. Your labels can be printed offset with gummed backs. They should have a homemade look to them which will reinforce the impression of the small-kitchen nature of your operation. If your food specialty does not spoil easily, your investment is that much safer. Relishes and other preserved goods in particular have a long shelf life.

Bring your goods to the retail outlets and try to get paid upon delivery. The less billing you have to do, the less expense you have to incur, and the more likely you are to avoid uncollectable debts. Most small one-person businesses do not have either the facilities or the money to go after nonpayers. Make sure when pricing your goods, regardless of whom you sell them to, that you are getting at least 40 percent profit over and above your cost for materials. If you develop the facility for turning out your product quickly, your time will be handsomely rewarded.

27 · Home Repair Service

When most people want a wall painted, pictures hung, a ceiling fixture installed, or a new wall where one did not exist before, they do not feel capable of performing that task by themselves. This is especially true of older or retired people. If you are physically able, you do not have to be a skilled carpenter, electrician or plumber to perform minor home repairs.

Yet most people, when they think of having home repairs performed, feel they have to go to a contracting service, and it is likely that the charges will be substantial for such a service. If you have even a hobbyist's knack with tools, you can advertise that you do minor home repairs at reasonable rates, and you could find yourself in full-time business quite quickly.

Make it understood to a prospective client that your home repair service is limited to simple carpentry (such as making bookcases), light fixture installation, picture and mirror hanging, painting, even minor plumbing repairs (such as fixing a leaky faucet). Older homeowners, in particular, will be one of your most lucrative markets. Advertise your service boldly but tastefully in the classified section of the newspaper. List the specific services you perform rather than just a general "Home Repair Service."

Your fees will be based on your time plus the cost of materials. Once you are in business you can talk to a local home building supplier and impress upon the supplier that you are a professional and would like to receive a professional discount in return for giving the supplier your exclusive business. You should, of course, have your own tools, which may require an initial investment of as much as $100. But if you have lived in a house for any length of time it is likely you already possess most of the tools you will need for this trade, such as a hammer, screwdrivers, wrenches, a drill and a selection of small hardware.

Aside from tools, anything you must buy from a building supplier to complete the job should be billed extra. It will be up to you whether you want to add on to your "wholesale" cost for materials. You should get at least $5 to $8 an hour for your time. Bear in mind that skilled carpenters, electricians and plumbers frequently command in excess of $15 an hour for their time.

Home repair service, although not really seasonal, is done most frequently in the spring and summer months. Carpenters, electricians and plumbers find that the winter season brings little work. Therefore you will probably have more competition in the colder months. When a client has asked you to come over to discuss a project, go with the notion that you might be suggesting other projects to your client at the same time. For instance, if you are called in to do minor renovations for a child's room, you might also suggest that the client consider a low-cost platform bed or double-decker beds to create more available play space.

Of course, your "overhead" for this business should not include any kind of facility except a desk and telephone in your home. Your work will be done exclusively outside. As your business grows, you will be in a position to hire a staff of part-time helpers who may not need your degree of skill but who can be very helpful with asistance on the job (at a lower scale of pay). It is possible to develop this business to the point where it can net you as much as $25,000 a year or more.

28 · Public Relations

The purpose of a public relations agency is to create and maintain a favorable image for its clients. Frequently this is misunderstood. Many people think public relations is a luxury limited to large corporations, Hollywood stars or politicians. But nothing could be further from the truth. Every business that sells anything, regardless of its size, wants to enhance its public image.

The service itself involves writing press releases, preparing booklets emphasizing one aspect of a company or individual, writing speeches and making films, editing an employee publication such as "in house" newspapers, and placing articles favorable to the client in newspapers. Public relations can also include promotion, setting up special events, getting guest speakers for groups, and other such services. Advertising promotion promotes a company's product. Public relations promotes the company itself.

Public relations (or press relations as it is sometimes called) is a service that many individuals and companies would utilize if they were aware of what the service can offer.

For instance, a company that manufactures plastic food containers would find it advantageous to promote the idea of storing food in plastic containers. This is over and above the sales of their particular product. As a public relations service person in this case, you might be called on to research articles on the efficiency of storing in plastic containers versus jars or wrapping. It could be your job to map a public relations campaign, which would include the placement of news articles (not advertising) in the so-called public interest. You might be called on to examine government research papers that show that food stored in plastic containers actually has a longer storage life. You might also prepare talks or articles on how inexpensive plastic containers have become in recent years. Where possible, you will mention the name of the company for whom you are working as a public relations servant, but the main purpose of your job is to create a favorable public image for the company itself.

A local political candidate, whose needs may be only for the duration of an election campaign, might find great value in your service on a temporary basis. It would be your job to act as liaison between the press and the candidate. Obviously, with success this can lead to a possible appointment as press officer if this candidate is elected.

The basic idea when putting together your public relations service is to keep in mind that you must map a P.R. campaign in *advance*. What to the public may just look like the chance appearance of an article in a newspaper really should be part of a well-coordinated effort to publicize your client or his company. You should be able to offer a virtual well-spring of ideas that can enhance your client's image.

Your fee should be based on an hourly rate as a "consultant." If the opportunity is available, try to get a monthly retainer from a client. Depending on the intensity of the P.R. effort, your fee should run from between $100 to $600 a month, plus expenses.

If you are dealing on a temporary basis for a client, or even just one publicity campaign, do not try to figure out exactly how many hours it will take you in advance. First, map out your strategy, draw a general idea of what amount of time is involved and give your client an approximation of the fee. Leave room in your fee so that you can be compensated for unexpected expenditures of time and money.

A public relations service does not depend necessarily on an investment in materials, except perhaps a typewriter and a telephone. Your largest expense will be one of time, both in consulting with your client and in furthering his or her image. One client should not require an average of more than one or two days a week. You can assume as many jobs as you can handle yourself. Once your business is under way you can consider a secretarial staff as well as other assistants, but do not rush into hiring anyone right away.

Avoid taking on competitive clients, so that your public relations efforts do not overlap. People who have become adept in the P.R. business can command fees that net them as much as $50,000 or more per year. Your beginning in this business should be directed toward those areas such as local political candidates, small to medium corporations in your area, and others whom you can service as an individual (at an obviously lower rate than a heavyweight P.R. firm).

Your service will be based on the fact that you can give your client personal attention without the need for massive outlays of cash. The success of your public relations service will depend on the energy you can devote to each client rather than the amount of money you need to spend.

29 · Business Services

There is hardly an organization in this country that does not have a need at some time or other for typed letters, bills and purchase orders, as well as other office services. The only training basically needed to provide this service is an ability to type quickly. Of course you should have a typewriter of your own, preferably an electric model with a carbon ribbon. If you don't own a typewriter, you can rent one, usually for about $25 a month (and in many cases this rental can be applied toward the purchase).

Running a business service from your home has many advantages. First, of course, you do not have to rent an office. Secondly, it is the kind of work that can be done part-time during the day, or even at night. So if you hold another job or want to earn a part-time income, you can start with very little difficulty.

The first and best way to solicit business is to announce your service in a local classified ad. College newspapers and public-announcement bulletin boards are also good places to advertise, since students, writers and teachers frequently need a large amount of typing and just do not have the time, or perhaps the skill, to do their own work. In your classified ad you should emphasize the speed and reliability of your service, but leave the setting of rates until you actually see the work that has to be done.

Figure your time on the basis of about $3 per hour, in addition to materials. If you are supplying the paper for the typing job, this should be added to your fee. In the brochure you prepare for public announcements, especially if you are placing them in college communities, put your service rates right up on the board. Usually you will charge by the page for longer work, such as manuscripts, theses and business letters. Be specific in your announcements. Let your customers know that for, say, 75¢ per page, they will receive an original plus one carbon, double spaced. Charge extra for envelopes if the customer wants these. A rate of 8¢ per envelope would not be unusual.

If you have worked as a secretary and can take dictation, then you have a valuable additional service to offer. You can, in this case, charge by the hour. And you can expect to do much of your work in the client's office.

A rate of $5 per hour for dictation and transcription is about average. Your rate schedule for specialized jobs will depend on the work needed. If, for instance, you are required to draw or type graphs and charts, you should charge approximately one-third higher than for straight typing.

Once you establish a list of clients whom you can service conveniently, you might find yourself in a position to accept a regular retainer for a certain number of hours spent each week at a client's office. Many small businesses find it advantageous to use the same service repeatedly since it can be expected that you will get to know the client's needs better and better as you go along.

In addition to typing and dictation you can offer a record-keeping service, in which case you should charge your hourly rate of $5. This service might involve tabulating receipts from a given business and entering them in a record book. It might even involve a simplified form of bookkeeping. You could even offer a complete office service, including the preparation and sending out of correspondence, bills, checks and the like. Your rates will depend pretty much on how much time is spent, since your client should provide materials for most jobs.

In addition to classified advertising and public announcements, you would do well to personally solicit business from organizations who might not have even thought of using an outside service. For instance, some organizations like PTAs and charitable groups may have a need for business services only once in a while. Make sure that the secretary of an organization knows you are available for work on a spontaneous basis.

If you are supplying the paper and copies for your client, make sure you use a reasonably good bond and have a good typewriter ribbon. If mistakes occur, use erasers or "Ko-Rec-Type" carefully. The success of your business will depend, in great part, on your speed and efficiency. If you have a deadline for a client, by all means go to great extremes to meet that deadline. As with any service business, your reliability is the prime requisite. Once your business has grown to the point where you can afford larger expenditures for advertising, you should consider placing a small classified ad in specialty magazines, such as *Writer's Digest*, and even scientific or technical publications. Using national publications for your advertisements, of course, means that you will be doing business by mail. If you are dealing with a company of some size, ask that a purchase order be sent for the amount of work you estimate the company will be sending. If you are doing work for individual writers or students, get a small deposit at the time the work is submitted and send your bill for the remainder of the work at the time the work is completed. Dealing by mail can be risky if you are not careful. On the other hand, it can provide you with a nationwide market for your service.

30 · Music Teacher

If you are an accomplished musician or singer, you already possess the raw materials to begin your own music teaching business. But even if you are not an accomplished performer, you still may have a lucrative market just by gaining a familiarity with a musical instrument. Depending on your degree of skill, you can teach adult musicians or children who just want an introduction to music on a particular instrument. Bear in mind that you don't have to be the best performer but you do have to know how to impart information to your students.

A small regular advertisement in your local newspaper can bring satisfactory results. You can charge as much as $5 for a half-hour private lesson, in which case your income could grow substantially with part-time devotion. You do not need a studio to give music lessons. You can use your own living room, as long as you can be sure you will have privacy during the lesson. At a rate of anywhere from $8 to $10 an hour for private instruction, you can see that an income of $200 a week, working by yourself, is an attainable goal.

You can also offer lessons to small groups. This is especially effective for an introduction to music for children. Five youngsters, at a cost to them of $2 an hour per child, will bring you the same kind of income as the more arduous private lesson.

People who instruct in the playing of an instrument are frequently asked for recommendations about the kind of instrument to buy, new or used. It would pay for you to contact one or more music stores in your area and get them to service your students, and give you a commission for sending customers to them. This aspect of your business alone can grow to the point where you could become a wholesale supplier of musical instruments.

When your teaching business has grown sufficiently, it then will be time to consider taking on additional staff. This does not mean you have to hire a studio. If you can coordinate spacing properly, you can use one or two rooms in your house or apartment to serve as many as fifteen or twenty students a day.

You would also do well to visit local schools and leave advertising material for distribution. Frequently, students who start music lessons in public school want to continue with private lessons afterward. If you can establish a relationship with a music department you would have a ready source of new students. (You might even want to consider hiring the public school music teacher as one of your staff teachers for work after school.)

31 · Firewood Supply

This is a business that can be developed with a small investment in tools and a large investment in elbow grease. The appeal of a crackling fire in a fireplace on a cold day is something most people can't resist. But firewood, especially in larger cities, is very hard to come by and can be expensive. You can benefit from this "inflated" market by having your own station wagon or van and a power chain saw (rented if you don't own one).

If you live in a rural community, chances are you have an abundant source of supply for firewood. You can visit various farmers or others with wooded property in the area and offer to clear the owner's land of dead wood. Load up your vehicle with wood cut to size (pieces should be no longer than three feet). Stock your firewood in the warm seasons and sell it at very attractive prices in the fall.

Depending on the area in which you live, a cord of wood will sell from $45 to $100. And this does not include stacking the wood for the customer. What you do is bring a cord of wood to your customer and unload it in a designated place. It is usually up to the customer to stack the wood neatly. You can offer to stack as an additional service, in which case you add a cost of at least $8 per cord for that work.

If you live near a large city, you might find that it pays to take the trip with a load of firewood, which you then sell right from your vehicle. In New York it is not uncommon to see a peddler of firewood standing near his station wagon selling three-foot logs for as much as $1 each.

How much can you make in this business? Virtually as much as your energy and time allow. If you are acquiring your firewood at little or no cost, then obviously the price you charge will be totally for your time and your equipment.

If a cord of wood sells for $75 and it takes you two hours to chop and stack that wood, and another hour and a half to deliver it, you can see that your profit can amount to as much as $20 or more. From this gross income you must draw your fuel expenses for delivery and then rental of a chain saw, if you don't already own one. But a quick calculation should show you that even working a seasonal business like this can provide you with a tidy sum of money. Some firewood suppliers earn enough in six months to take care of their needs for the rest of the year.

32 · Shut-In Visiting Service

As the medical ability to prolong life has grown in recent decades, so has one of the most severe problems that we hear least about. It is the care of aged people. Everyone undoubtedly knows a grandparent or elderly person who needs not only physical attention but help in overcoming the problems of loneliness.

For those who can afford it, nursing homes are one answer to this problem. Recent scandals in the nursing home industry, however, turned many people who have money away from this solution. A business that you could begin with virtually no overhead, and gain great satisfaction from, is a "shut-in" visiting service. There are virtually thousands and thousands of elderly or handicapped people who are not sick enough to demand full-time medical attention, but who cannot for obvious reasons perform many normal day-to-day functions by themselves. It is true that welfare agencies supply some help to these unfortunate people. But the reading of any newspaper will prove that there are great numbers of older people, especially in large cities, who are "invisible citizens."

If you have your own transporation you can visit these people, do their shopping for them, or even just sit and talk to them. The children of many of these shut-ins would willingly pay a moderate amount for this service. Your rates would compare favorably with anything approaching full-time help, and you could provide a warm ray of light to the drab lives these people lead.

Offer you service by placing 8½ x 11 mimeographed announcements on bulletin boards in churches, "Y"s, retirement societies, golden age groups, virtually any place that older people might gather for one reason or another. Your fees should be based on a per-visit rate. If you are visiting someone's home two or three or even four times a week, you can charge up to $5 a visit, assuming it will last longer than about one hour. But even a few hours a week could be considered precious time to these people who are not as mobile as they would like to be. The service you render in doing errands or even reading short passages from a book will not only be important to these shut-ins but will also be an invaluable service to your community. If you put together a schedule of six to eight visits a day, you could easily clear $200 a week or more.

Classified advertisements, of course, are helpful. But your service will probably be more sought after by those who see bulletins posted by local social groups.

In addition to a private service you should check with your local welfare agency to see if they wish to pay you to perform this service for them. Frequently local charitable groups, if they don't have their own funding, have received government grants to promote such a service.

This is not a business in which you will grow to become a large corporation. It is, however, a business which could net you a very nice profit and it can be done part-time, even in the evenings and on weekends.

It is safer to start a business like this while you hold a job. It is easy to find out how big a list of clients you could develop without actually committing yourself to full-time work.

If you enjoy helping people, if you find satisfaction in doing something very useful in the community, then this business could provide you with a feeling of accomplishment much greater than any money you will receive.

33 · Salvage-Supply Service

Here is an extremely high-potential-profit business for those people who love to make deals. The way it works is this: You find out who is going out of business, especially retail stores and small offices. You also find out, by checking death notices, what estates might be up for auction soon. You are, of course, capitalizing on someone's grief when one of these situations occurs.

People, whether they be heirs to a small estate or the hapless owners of a failed business, are in a position where their goal is to acquire cash quickly and not be burdened with the responsibility for storing and transporting either household goods or business supplies.

The object is to get there first and make a single offer for the complete contents of a house or business. You can expect to get the complete contents at bargain rates, sometimes as much as 90 percent less than if the goods were sold individually. You'll find it much easier to cut a deal if you come prepared to pay cash, greenbacks. Salvage-supply operators can make fortunes almost overnight with the right buy. Don't count on becoming rich tomorrow, but you can, with wise buying, acquire very valuable, sometimes nearly new, goods for a song.

Now once you have acquired the contents of a house or business, what do you do? If you have set up a number of contacts with used business supply stores, used furniture stores, antique shops and other dealers in "secondhand" merchandise, you might be able to arrange to sell your goods before you even buy them. In this case you are acting as a distributor, a middleman (and "middleman" fees can be enormous, just check with any lawyer who handles probate work).

If you haven't sold all the goods you purchase at bargain prices you should be ready to store them. You'll need a van, although a rented trailer you put on the back of your car could do, and you will need a space to store goods that have not sold immediately. If you could use your garage and you don't have too many large items to store, your cost would be nothing. But even if you have larger items you don't have to rent space in a large warehouse.

Frequently people rent out their garages for storage for others. It means, of course, going from place to place (and the object would be to have as much merchandise in one storage place as possible). But you can arrange to have goods of a distinct type, such as dishes, silverware and household accessories, stored in one place, while you have larger furniture stored in another place. You can rent one or more garages for as little as $30 to $40 a month, depending on rental rates in your area.

Your job, once you salvage goods from a business or estate, is to sort out the material. The more awareness you have of the value of antiques the better you can recognize values in the property you acquire. You also have to develop a facility for pricing a whole room full of goods quickly. This means that you should know, for instance, what a used desk can sell for, or what you can get for a typewriter or file cabinet or even boxes of scrap stationery.

Don't forget junkyards as a possible outlet for your goods. Estate sales often include one or more old cars which may not have run for years. Arrange with a salvage yard to cart away junk goods for a prearranged rate. If you're willing to work at it yourself you can even rent a tow truck and work directly with an automobile junkyard that specializes in selling used-car parts.

If you are buying the contents of a building for what you have calculated to be 10 percent of the going price, you should be able to sell all those goods over a period of time for an average of 40 percent of the going price.

Most privately owned, large salvage businesses started very modestly. Usually a person went and searched for goods that could be purchased for a fraction of their value and sold those goods for a profit. It is probably the simplest of all capitalistic enterprises. Yet if you ever met a successful junk dealer you might be surprised from his elegant appearance that he deals in discarded goods. Successful junkyards are one of the most profitable businesses around.

The salvage-supply business has probably more growth potential now than in recent years. People are frequently looking for used items instead of spending money on new goods. Of course, anything you discover of antique value will bring additional profit beyond the normal mark-up for goods that you salvage.

You will have to have an initial amount of cash to buy out a distressed business or estate. But if you have been energetic you should be able to more than make back this money within a week.

It is not necessarily a business you have to borrow to get into, but if you have anywhere from $500 on up to spend, your risk is really quite small. Try to manage as much of this business as you can by yourself. If you pick up the goods from one place and deliver them to another, hire a part-time helper. The more you do for yourself the more money you will have to spend on an investment in profit-producing goods.

34 · Small-Business Consultant

A good way to capitalize on your background, if you have been a business person, is to give help for a fee to others who need the advice of an experienced business person.

Solicit your clients from those areas you know well. If you were a successful retailer, go to small stores in your town that might find your assistance very valuable. If you were a financial consultant you can offer your service as an investment counselor to families. The same could hold true if you had a background in advertising or public relations. There are literally hundreds of small firms started by inexperienced people who could benefit greatly from advice by one who has experience in their business.

Start your business with an advertisement that says something like: "Is Your Business Hurting? Successful Retailer [broker] [advertising executive] Available for Consultation. Flexible Fee."

Your fees will actually depend on the size and volume of the business you are assisting. If you help a small retailer buy goods more efficiently, or advertise successfully, then you would have to figure your rates in the area of $10 an hour. If, on the other hand, a large corporation calls you to assist in a public relations campaign, your fee can be as high as $50 an hour. You could manage to net $300 to $400 each week. You'll find that as you become more adept at consulation and as your list of clients (satisfied, of course) grows, your service will be in demand through word-of-mouth advertising as much as anything else.

To solicit your first account don't be embarrassed to walk right into somebody's store and strike up a conversation about the business. Most small retailers, unless they think you are a spy, enjoy talking about their business. And you might discover ways in which you can be helpful immediately.

To gain access to larger corporations you should set up interviews with the people who specialize in the area you wish to consult about. Your investment should consist of a moderate supply of business cards and letterheads.

Your billing, especially if you can get a consultation contract for a period of time, will be monthly. You can even begin this business by consulting evenings and weekends while you hold you present job. Avoid the risk of simply leaving one job to start business cold. Do as much research as you can into the need for your service. Take the time to solicit clients you can service during nonbusiness hours. This will not be difficult with such businesses as small retailers who will be most available for consultation while they are not working at the store.

Just be sure to stay as close as possible to areas in which you are already an expert. The consulting business is not one which you can learn as you go along.

35 · Blade Sharpening

The need for sharp lawnmowers, knives and other cutting tools is one which does not come often in the average household. But when it is necessary, it is a vital service. This is a business in which you can become an independent contractor as well as a direct service person to the public. Your investment will require the acquisition of some sharpening machinery, which can be paid out over a period of time.

For lawnmower sharpening equipment you could go to someone like the Foley Mfg. Co. of Minneapolis. This company not only sells sharpening tools for rotary and reel-type lawnmowers but offers instruction in their use—either in person or by mail. Once you have acquired your machinery, such as grinding wheels, files, etc., you will be in a position to be open for business. You can use a basement or garage as a workshop, especially if you offer to pick up or deliver tools to be sharpened. Your fee, of course, will have to compensate you for the time necessary for the pickup and delivery.

You can begin getting accounts by advertising in a local paper. In addition, you should make it your business to visit hardware stores in your area. Leave your business cards and explain the service that you offer. Frequently, customers who buy cutlery will bring them back to the store for maintenance (or sharpening).

You could set up a contracting service to do all the sharpening service for a particular store. In this case you would make pickups once or twice a week at the store and return the sharpened tools the next day. Most retail outlets, and even some shops that sell power equipment, do not offer a sharpening service on the premises. It is something that is usually detail work for a store engaged in selling hundreds of items and it usually requires a skilled or at least experienced person to run this machinery.

Offer to assist in any advertising for the stores you get contracts from by preparing posters which could be placed near the tools and cutlery section. Talk also to those that sell power mowers, chain saws and other cutting equipment. These shops get a great deal of repair work but may be interested in a sharpening service. This means they can save money on maintenance of machinery and not take a man off a mechanical repair to sharpen blades.

To arrive at pricing for your service, check the going rates in your area. A rotary-type lawnmower usually costs between $6 and $10 to sharpen. You can get more for reel-type lawnmowers because the sharpening takes longer.

You'll find that your lawnmower sharpening business is seasonal. Ninety percent of your business, especially in the North, will be during a twelve-week spring-summer season. But don't limit yourself just to lawnmowers. People are using cutlery all the time, as well as hobby shop tools and other items that do not depend on outdoor use.

As your business grows, think about setting up your own *mobile* sharpening business. This has been done by others with the use of a refurbished school bus which can be purchased for a little as $500. You will not have to drive great distances, so you don't need a spanking-new efficient vehicle. Basically you need space, and old school buses seem to fill this bill very well. You then can go from shopping center to shopping center on a given day each week. People will know when you are coming and will be ready. Announce your schedule in the newspaper as well as on posters you place on bulletin boards in supermarkets and other stores willing to let you advertise.

Of course, with your own sharpening equipment on your own truck you could branch as widely, geographically, as you choose. You might even find it profitable to visit neighboring towns, say, on a once-a-month basis.

The profit potential in this business is moderate. You could net several hundred dollars a week, but it is more likely that you'll find you are working very long hours in the summer and short hours in the winter.

Think of expanding your business, once it's under way, by instituting a tool reconditioning business. This simply means having a minimum set of tools which you can use to tighten screws and do minor repairs on cutlery.

36 · Backgammon/Bridge/Chess Lessons

There has been a resurgence of home entertainment in recent years and one of the most popular home games is backgammon. Bridge, of course, has been a steady card game for decades, and chess has caught the popular imagination, thanks in great part to Bobby Fischer's antics.

For families addicted to television there has been a desire to learn and improve skills in these games on a scale that this country has never seen before. Backgammon sets, for instance, with prices as high as $300 a set, are selling like hotcakes in many large cities. Backgammon is not a complicated game but does have several levels of strategy which make it more intriguing than many dice games. Obviously, if you are going to give lessons in one of these games you should be a good player yourself. Of the three popular games here, backgammon is far and away garnering the greatest appeal right now. It is also the simplest game to learn. There are several books available on the subject which outline the simple rules and object of the game. If you were to try to learn one of these games from scratch, backgammon should be the one to choose. You can become good at this game in a relatively short period of time.

Whichever game you specialize in, however, the methods for setting up a teaching business are the same. Begin by advertising lessons in a classified ad in the paper, but don't run too many ads before doing anything else. Check in your town to see if there is a local backgammon, bridge or chess club. Almost every town has at least one. And if there is not one in your area, or if the clubs that do exist do not seem satisfactory, you can set your own club up with no investment.

Start your ad or poster with words like "Learn Winning Backgammon [Bridge] [Chess] In Six Easy Lessons." Set up to teach no more than six to ten individuals at a time. Of course, if we are talking about bridge, the number of students should be divisible by four. For group lessons you can charge up to $2 per hour for each student, for a single lesson. Thus, one hour's work in an evening can net you $20.

You can hold lessons at your own home or at a hall sponsored by an organization. You do not need a great deal of space. You do need tables for the players and as many sets of games as you have students. For bridge, acquiring several decks is not an expense worth noting. But for backgammon and chess you should get moderately good sets that cost less than $10 each. Backgammon will be your most expensive investment since the games usually start at $5 or more for a decent set. But you could start with several dime-store sets, although they will not last too long.

You can offer private instruction and for this you should get $10 per hour. You can even offer to visit a student's home. And remember, this is an especially good business to run in the evening.

Once you have acquired students for your classes, you're in a good position to start a club, or even more important, to set up tournaments.

Tournaments can be of any size you wish. You should charge a small entry fee and offer prizes. You can offer cash prizes or you can solicit local merchants for donations of merchandise at reduced prices. Aside from your advertising, your only investment in a tournament (after you pay for your prizes) is the mimeographed sheets of the rules, as well as a poster on which you write down the winners at each level of the tournament.

Tournaments are an excellent way to publicize your service. One man even went to a local restaurant and got them to sponsor a backgammon tournament on a Wednesday evening (when the restaurant was doing little business). For a fee, say $20, the entrants not only paid to participate in the tournament but for refreshments supplied by the restaurant. It turned out to be a very good promotional device for the restaurant and the backgammon teacher, and is now a regular feature there. With tournaments giving you a profit, and lessons in which you are paid for your time, you could easily net $200 a week or more.

This business can be run effectively in the evening, particularly because it is a form of recreation that people enjoy during their leisure hours. You need not even leave your current job to set it up.

As your business develops you may also sell games as a wholesaler. This means buying supplies from a manufacturer (obviously backgammon and chess will be your higher profit items) and selling these to your students. Become an expert in your area in backgammon, bridge or chess, and people will begin to find you.

37 · Specialty Auto Repair

If you have had experience as a mechanic, or if you know a good mechanic whom you can go into partnership with, there is a type of auto repair business for you that has grown remarkably in recent years.

Foreign car manufacturers have franchised dealers throughout the country, but not nearly as many as the American manufacturers have. If you've ever owned a foreign car you might have realized how difficult it was to get good service for it. Most owners of foreign cars are reluctant to take them to just any gas station or dealer who does not specialize in that type of car. If there were a place, a small garage preferably, that dealt with, let's say, Volkswagens, there would be much less reluctance to bring the car there for normal service, especially service after the warranty has expired.

Although you may have to rent space to service a particular foreign car, you might also use your own garage or even a vacant lot. Check the zoning requirements in your area for setting up this business near your home. Advertise that you specialize in Volkwagens or Datsuns or Toyotas. Do not offer service for more than one make at a time. Stress that you give quick, good service on this particular kind of car and that your service is limited only to, say, Volkswagens. This will give customers the feeling that you are indeed a specialist in their vehicle. With the hundreds of thousands of Volkswagens currently running on the roads of this country there are far too few authorized dealers to take care of the repair demand. The same is true, to a lesser extent, for Datsun, Toyota and Fiat.

If you are a mechanic, or partners with one, you should already have most of the tools necessary for auto repair. You don't need a hydraulic lift or anything enormously expensive like that.

Your charge for repair service is on a basis of $15 to $20 an hour, plus the cost of parts. This will take care of overhead and salaries. You can make a profit on parts. Have an arrangement with a nearby supplier of parts for that car so that you can purchase goods wholesale. You do not have to stock a complete inventory of parts, as would a dealer, especially if you are near enough to pick up parts on a daily basis. The biggest lag between starting your business and profiting from it will come during the time you are trying to get customers. If you have been a mechanic with a foreign car dealer, or if you are in partnership with such a mechanic, it's very possible the mechanic will already have a following of his own. Specialized foreign car repair is like the hairdressing business—in terms of sticking with someone whose work you like. It is not unusual for people to go to a particular mechanic rather than a particular garage.

An aspect of your business that can be developed later is the customizing business. There have been successful businesses built on supplying Volkswagen customizing equipment, such as fiber glass fronts and rears (to make the Volkswagen look like a squashed Rolls-Royce), as well as different equipment to improve the efficiency and speed of the vehicle. The important point to remember, especially when starting out, is to specialize in one type of car only.

38 · Needlework Decoration

The clothing industry in this country has undergone a radical change within the past few years. The trend has been away from more formal wear, especially in men's clothing, to a much more casual approach. Even employees of large corporations now can be seen in the corridors in pant suits and leisure wear. Young people in patricular have been the cause of a great upsurge in the denim business, to the point of having created a large industry in used jeans. Manufacturers caught on to the appeal of washed-out denim and have started to "prewash" denim so that it looks used.

One of the ways that a number of people achieve individuality with their clothing is to have it decorated, either with appliqué or embroidery, and this goes for men too. Everyone by now has probably seen a needlework-decorated jean jacket, slacks or shirt. The popularity of this custom needlework business in growing. Manufacturers have even started doing appliqué work in their stitching factories. But it is no substitute for a *custom* needle-decorated item of clothing.

If you have minimal sewing skill, you can purchase an interesting piece of print fabric for, say, $2.50 a yard. By cutting out a pattern from this print you could decorate as many as eight or ten pairs of jeans. And once you establish a facility for applying these print fabrics to clothing you should be able to do as many as two or three an hour. Selling your service for $10 per garment means, of course, that you can have an income of $20 an hour or more with an expenditure of less than 50¢ a garment (if you have your own sewing machine). If you don't have your own machine you can rent one and the renting fee is usually applied against the purchase price.

But you don't even have to have a machine to do needlework. There is a great demand for embroidery of all types done by hand. Patterns are available, though you can also draw your own pictures, which you fill in with different-colored thread to decorate a piece of clothing. This kind of needlework takes much longer than anything done on a machine and will have to be priced accordingly. It could take you five hours to decorate one jacket, in which case you should get a minimum of $25 to $30 for your work.

You can do needlework at home even in your spare time. It is a good source of income because there is so little cash outlay for materials. The customers provide the garments themselves. Advertise in a local newspaper that you do custom needlework decoration and show a picture of your work if possible.

An even more potentially profitable plan is to go to Army/Navy stores in your area as well as those stores that specialize in casual slacks and other items. Bring a sample of your work to the store and let them display it to their customers. You can then go to the store as many times a week as necessary to pick up work. Your fee to the store will be the same as to individual direct customers, and the merchant will add that fee on to the cost of the goods.

Another outlet for your talent: Design needlework patterns and sell them as a hobby kit. You put together the proper amount of thread and the sewing needles necessary to complete the work, as well as the muslin or other material on which needlework will be applied.

Of course, you can make other things besides decorative clothing. You can make pillows, throws and other goods.

You charge by the garment or item you are going to decorate. In the case of a needlework pillow or other complicated design work, figure your time in advance. Be careful when looking at a design to calculate carefully how long it will take you to complete the work. A simple design can be deceiving. Your business can net you $150 or more a week, even spending only part of your time. How quickly you want your business to grow will be dictated by the time you want to spend.

39 · Household Budget Consultant

Personal bankruptcies are being filed at a larger rate than at any time in the past forty years. Many, many thousands of American families are finding themselves in debt way beyond their means and with little hope of paying back those bills in a reasonable amount of time. The stress from being bombarded by collection agencies is more than most people want to tolerate. But most people don't know where to turn, except when it's too late.

If you have "a head for figures," or you have had good experience managing your own household budget, you might qualify to act as a budget consultant for other families. This is a business which can be run on a one-person basis and has great potential. Most accounting and legal firms cannot take on individual private clients at reasonable fees because they are geared for heavy-duty corporate work or business consultation.

Begin with a classified ad that reads something like, "Money Troubles At Home? Will Help You Get Out Of Debt Without Borrowing." Any family in deep financial trouble will reach for a service like this as if they were reaching for a life raft. In exchange for a fee that compensates you for your time, at the rate of about $10 to $15 per hour, you can become the voice of wisdom and salvation to these families.

It will be your job to show a family, after looking at all their expenses and all their income, how they can manage on the income they currently have. If the family is in debt way over its head you can advise on how to pay off these debts over a longer period of time without incurring penalties or lawsuits. As you may already know, companies that are owed money are most anxious to hear from their debtors even if it means collecting the money over a longer period of time. Frequently a third party, such as a consultant, writing letters to a family's creditors can get an extension on debts that will allow the family to climb back to solvency without losing everything they have.

You may have to advise people to take strong medicine. You may even have to suggest that a family sell its house or car, or even file for bankruptcy. You would do well to associate yourself with a local attorney who can handle private or personal bankruptcies.

You can offer your service through the newspaper, as mentioned, or through social groups which can place announcements of your service at their local headquarters, or even announce the availability of your service at organization meetings.

Another way to promote your service is to offer to speak before local groups on household budget management or even household investments. Social groups are frequently looking for speakers on interesting topics, and economic crisis is nothing if not an interesting topic. Come prepared to hand out business cards to those who may want to consider your service.

You should read several books on household budget management and you should put together your own simple manual that will apply to most household budget situations. There are many books on the market. You can design your own after interviewing several clients so that it suits the particular needs of your area.

You do not need a license to practice this kind of consulting work. Nor do you need special bonding or insurance. In fact, your only investment is your time. The expertise you develop and the success you have in helping clients will become your stock in trade.

40 · Art Instruction

Of course the basic prerequisite here is that you are an artist, or you at least qualify as one who can draw. You don't have to be an extremely accomplished artist but you should be able to communicate the rudiments of art to your students. If you are not an accomplished artist yourself you might consider limiting your instruction to children.

Advertise classes in your local newspaper as well as at churches and the local "Y." You should charge $1.50 to $2 per student per hour of lessons, and you should be able to take as many as ten students at one time.

Before venturing to other organizations to sponsor art lessons you'd best be advised to have a couple of series of home lessons under your belt. Draw posters emphasizing "Learn To Draw." With several classes a day of either group or private instruction (for which you should get a minimum of $10 an hour) you could net as much as $200 a week or more. For many artists who have always wanted more freedom to pursue their own creative output this is a good way to make money and get that freedom at the same time. If you have a background in advertising or commercial art you can adjust your art instruction to emphasize what you know best. There will be a sizable market for art instruction if you can show that this talent might lead to work in industry.

Design a poster that illustrates some of the work of your students. When someone sees a beautiful picture drawn by a friend or relative, it will be an incentive for them to say, "Well I can do that too."

Your lessons should be held once a week for each class. Try to make the timing correspond to public school scheduling and you will not have any problem dealing with the holidays.

Your fee should not include artists' materials. You should have places with easels and tables for students to work. Give them a list of supplies they should purchase and expect them to bring their own art tools, including paper or canvas. You net income will be based solely on the time involved, rather than any materials you might need. You can buy portable easels, either used or new, reasonably inexpensively. For children you can use inexpensive card tables or even the floor as a work surface.

If you are working from your home studio, especially with children, be ready to deal with lots of paint splatters and clutter. Above all, make your classes fun and you should get plenty of repeat business.

41 · Gourmet Cooking Classes

Almost everyone who watches television is aware of Julia Child and Graham Kerr, the Galloping Gourmet. These are just two of the well-known personalities who almost single-handedly have brought gourmet cooking into the average American home. And now more and more people want to learn how to cook Chinese food, or French food, or other national delicacies that cannot easily be manufactured by the mass food marketers. If you have a penchant for cooking and if you enjoy it, you can become expert in any specialized cuisine simply by getting a good cookbook and practicing making those dishes.

Once you have acquired a moderate amount of gourmet skill, or if you already possess that skill, you could be in great demand to teach it to others. It can be done right from your own kitchen with small groups and requires no more investment than a small ad to set up your classes. Advertise that you are offering a short course in, say, "French cuisine." You can handle as many as six to eight people in one class.

Each class should feature one dish which you select in advance. Mimeograph the complete ingredients and recipe for the dish before your class begins. Give these out to your students. The purpose of the class, of course, is for the students to learn some of the tricks of the trade, the little nuances that never get expressed properly in the cookbooks. Gourmet cooking, in particular, requires personal supervision. Also, of course, practicing under the guidance of an expert (like you) is just more fun than trial and error alone. You may need to acquire several sets of cooking implements, such as woks if you are instructing in Chinese cuisine, so that several members of the class can participate at the same time. The point is to let your students take part in the cooking, rather than just showing them. That is the advantage you have over Julia Child on television.

Either by personal solicitation or through your classified advertisement, get six to eight students to sign up for at least four lessons at one time. Each class should run from forty-five minutes to an hour and a half or more, depending how elaborate the recipe is.

In addition to knowing how to cook a particular kind of cuisine, be prepared to answer questions about the terminology used and other bits of information that will be valuable to your students.

If you have the time to hold two or three classes a day, your income can grow to be quite sizable. You should charge from $1.50 to $3 per person per lesson, and be sure to calculate the amount of food you will need to purchase for that class session. If you have six students at $2 each, and it costs you $3 for the ingredients, you have netted $9 for your cooking lesson. Two or three of these lessons each day can amount to $150 a week or more. Advertise that you let your students take home the things that they make. Also that you are willing to hold private lessons (for as much as $10 or more) for those students who wish very personal attention.

The growth potential for your business is really quite good. In addition to cooking lessons, you can hire yourself out as a cook for a particular occasion. If someone is throwing a party for fifty or sixty people and wants to have homemade gourmet delicacies served at this party, you can be hired as a visiting chef. You charge by the hour (from $5 to $10), and the cost of the food is of course the responsibility of the party host.

Running a gourmet cooking school at your home will give you credentials as a specialist in that type of cuisine. As your business grows you might find it advantageous to rent a large kitchen at a "Y" or church, or even a restaurant kitchen. You can also hire staff assistants who do not have to have your expertise in gourmet cuisine but can perform certain functions under your direction.

Also consider running gourmet cooking classes with the endorsement of different organizations. In that case you can expect that the organization will pay for the food and will collect the tuition. You should be paid on an hourly basis, a minimum of $5 an hour.

42 · Exterminator Service

Here is a competitive small business that offers good earnings for a relatively small investment of time. Pest control experts command fees that can be the equivalent of $30 an hour or more. Here's why: Exterminators are almost always called in when a property owner is under stress. When a homeowner is suddenly confronted by an attack from dozens of wasps nesting in his gutter, when an apartment dweller's kitchen is raided by an army of cockroaches—the first reaction is to call the exterminator, and hope that, unlike doctors, he makes housecalls at night.

When a pest control expert comes to your home at a moment's notice and eradicates the insects or rodents that were driving you crazy, you gladly pay his bill (so he'll come back quickly when you call him next time). His bill may be $25, and he may have spent only a half hour at your home. But his specialized service is really valuable when it is needed.

To go into this business requires that you have training in pest control. The best training would be to work with a licensed exterminator. Notice the word "licensed." Most states do issue licenses to pest control experts. If you want to see your business grow beyond a one-person operation, check with your state's Bureau of Consumer Affairs on licensing requirements. Although you can still practice as an exterminator without a license, you will eventually be limiting yourself. You will have an easier time getting bonded with a license. Without bonding you may have to take risks that could cost a great deal. When an exterminator performs a termite inspection, he usually states his findings in writing, especially if the inspection is in behalf of a prospective homeowner. If you make a mistake and the house is infested, you could be sued by the misled home buyer.

To start in the business, you can still solicit clients and do exterminating without a license. But work toward getting one as soon as possible. Join the National Pest Control Association, use brand-name products and advertise both these facts to your customer. (Many a small camera store has looked very important by using the Kodak brand name.)

Place a classified ad and a listing in the Yellow Pages that states specifically *all* the pest control services you can perform: fumigating, moth-proofing, squirrel control, rat-proofing, mice, bedbugs, cockroaches, ants, fleas, wasps, bees, etc. And, of course, termite control and inspection.

When you choose a name for your company, select one that starts with lots of "A's." The purpose is simple: to be listed as close as possible among the first in the category of "Exterminator" in the Yellow Pages. When people need emergency pest control help, they frequently call the first name they come to, alphabetically.

Become friendly with as many real estate brokers as you can. Brokers are often asked for recommendations from their home-buying clients for termite inspections. Most homes will not be finally sold until the prospective new owner is satisfied the house is free of termites. When the home buyer is new in the area, he or she relies heavily on the real estate broker for advice.

Your equipment, as a pest control expert, can be your car, station wagon or small van. Though you may have to carry fumigating equipment and other small machinery, you can fit just about everything in the trunk or back seat of a car. If you use your own automobile, you can turn it into a distinct advantage. Let your clients know that you use a regular automobile, with no company name printed on the vehicle, so that sensitive customers will not be embarrassed by a well-marked PEST CONTROL vehicle pulling up to their front door.

If your service to your customers is satisfactory you can depend on a great deal of repeat business. This seems to be a service in which strong client relationships play a very important part.

43 · *Self-Defense Instruction*

In large urban areas self-defense instruction has become more and more popular in recent years. Although self-defense is usually associated with one of the Oriental martial arts, like karate, judo or kung fu, the basic purpose of the instruction is really more devoted to warding off an attack by a street assailant than to the more spiritual aspect of these disciplines.

If you are a physical culturist, or even if you have simply studied one of the martial arts of boxing, you might be qualified to teach self-defense. If you have not practiced the art yourself, you should have little difficulty in finding a person who has, and in beginning a partnership with that person.

To start a self-defense school (or "Dojo" if you want to use the Oriental term), you can begin modestly, using a finished basement or any large room in your home. You should have mats on the floor, although you could make do with several carpets, one on top of the other, as a soft covering.

Advertise your school in local newspapers. At the same time, contact youth groups in public schools, "Y's" and even local health clubs and gyms. Unless you or your partner are a black belt, or some other highly ranked martial artist, you'd do best to publicize the *self-defense* benefits of your instruction. The classical study of a martial art is a long and arduous course to follow. By emphasizing pure self-defense, you are answering the most pressing need of people who want self-confidence when they find themselves in a threatening situation.

The appeal of self-defense instruction is not by any means limited to young men obsessed with *macho*. Children, starting as young as five years old, have become ardent enthusiasts (thanks in great part to television romantics), and women of all ages have long passed the stage of considering self-defense "unladylike."

For group classes you can charge from $1.50 to $4 per student, for classes of as many as ten or twelve. You don't need a calculator to figure out how much gross income that can mean for an hour's work.

Your expenses can be kept to a minimum. If you are using your own home, the savings are obvious. But even if you use the facilities of a "Y"' or health club, you need pay only a percentage of your receipts (no more than 35 percent). The one expense you should *not* avoid is insurance. More than most businesses, this one requires that you be covered for liability. Advertising that you have full insurance coverage will be reassuring to your students and their parents.

Keep your classes segregated, meaning separate women, men and children. Each will feel more comfortable. If you solicit women customers, it would pay to have a woman expert working with female students.

Although judo or karate outfits are not a necessity, they should be available, at the students' expense. To keep everyone's expenses to a minimum, you can begin by simply suggesting loose clothing, like sweatpants and sweatshirt. Once your classes are well established, you can sell martial arts costumes if you wish. You can profit from the sale of these items by working directly with a sporting goods supplier or manufacturer.

If your instruction tends toward the formal martial arts, you can also organize tournaments, perhaps even featuring guest experts. These tournaments can be an additional source of profit (by charging admission to family and friends of students) as well as a natural advertisement for your classes.

The growth potential of this business can be phenomenal. Many schools of self-defense have grown from one-room operations to franchised, nationwide chains in less than a year.

44 · Foreign Language Translator

If you are blessed with fluency in virtually any foreign language there are several ways to capitalize handsomely on your talent. Fluency does not mean you have to have studied the language formally for dozens of years. If you were simply lucky enough to grow up in a household where Spanish, French, Italian, Yiddish, Russian or any language other than English was spoken you are qualified to turn your bilingual ability into good money.

Translators, especially Spanish, are in great demand in schools and hospitals. Young non-English-speaking students need help desperately. Schools, elementary in particular, are employing Spanish-speaking adults who are not teachers but act as a teacher's aide. Hospitals have a constant call for second-language translators in sometimes life-and-death situations with emergency patients who do not speak enough English to tell a doctor what is wrong.

Then, of course, there are the more traditional needs for translators—for companies doing business overseas, for specialists who need foreign publications translated, as well as foreign language schools. Growing ethnic awareness in this country has led to an enormous demand among native Americans to learn the language of their forefathers.

Depending on what aspect of translation you have or wish to develop, your fees can net you from $50 a week for part-time work at home to hundreds of dollars a week for sophisticated business translations, sometimes involving scientific, technical translations.

As a free-lance translator, you can advertise your service in trade publications, scientific journals and large-city newspapers. The rates you can charge will vary with the difficulty of the work. If someone wants a popular German magazine article translated, your fee should be a minimum of $5 per hour. You may have to put your fee in terms of "per page," but just figure it carefully so you net not less than $5 an hour. For translating a scientific article in which you may need special knowledge in addition to second-language fluency, your fees can range up to $15 an hour.

You can also give classes in a foreign language, at your home, or private lessons. Small classes of students (not more than six or eight to a class) can net you $2 to $5 an hour per student. Private lessons should be as much as $10 per class. Students should pay for their own textbooks and other materials. (If you contact a foreign language publishing company yourself, you can make a modest profit on textbooks and, better yet, get good service on books you order directly. Unfortunately, most bookstores offer scant supplies of foreign language books, except for specialty stores in larger cities.)

Foreign language translation offers a wealth of opportunities to cash in on a unique talent, even if you already hold a full-time job you don't want to give up. Language classes can be and are frequently given in the evening. Free-lance translation of books and articles can easily be done evenings and weekends.

If you have a foreign-language typewriter (with foreign symbols and accent marks) you even have a market in serving European or Asian companies with U.S. offices. A typewriter, American or foreign, is about the only tool you'll need to invest in to start your business. How much and what type of work you get is only limited to the areas you want to solicit.

45 · Auto Driving School

If you are a good driver who does not get rattled easily under pressure, you have the minimum qualifications to start and run an auto driving school. Although you don't need much in the way of equipment besides a car with dual controls (a brake pedal on the passenger side of the car), you do have to have special auto insurance and, in most states, a special license. Anyone can teach someone else to drive a car, of course, without special licensing. But without a license you will be cutting off one of the chief attractions of professional driving instruction—namely, the reduced rates on insurance available to teen-agers who take lessons from an officially sanctioned school.

The best way to learn how auto driving instruction is given, even if you've had a spotless driving record for years, is to take a series of lessons from an already established school in your area. After you've experienced firsthand how it's done, check with your state's motor vehicle department for license and insurance requirements.

You can use your own car to teach. The dual control brake and possibly clutch pedals can be installed for less than $100 in most places.

Auto driving courses are usually broken into two parts: several hours of classroom instruction on how to pass the state's written exam, as well as driving techniques and on-the-road instruction. If you go into partnership with an experienced driving instructor, you can divide the work along those lines. You do the advertising, administration and classroom work; your partner does the on-the-road instruction. Except for classroom time, all driving instruction is private—just the teacher and student.

A course, usually consisting of two classroom hours and four to eight driving hours, commands fees of from $50 to $100 or more. You can attract students by advertising that you specialize in, for instance, teaching nervous or elderly students who may need extra confidence-building. Also promote the money savings on insurance available to teen-agers who complete the course. Offer free pickup and delivery service, as well as use of the school's car to take driving license tests (charge an extra flat fee for this use of your car).

Emphasize that your instruction is by mature, well-trained drivers who accompany students to the drivers' license test.

Even after paying the expenses to fuel and maintain your teaching vehicle, you can net several hundred dollars a week with a moderate to full teaching load. The state motor vehicle department will, in all likelihood, provide you with a generous supply of free instruction booklets which students study in anticipation of the written test.

You can also offer refresher courses in those states that require retesting of drivers every few years. When you calculate your fees, base them, first of all, on the prevailing rates in your area, and secondly, so that you net at least $7 to $8 an hour after expenses.

You can use your home as a combination teaching center and office. If you are in this business alone, you should engage an answering service to take calls from prospective students. If the answering service is able, have them make appointments and quote rates where possible.

Once you have worked with several students who have passed their driving tests, you will have established a proven record of success. You should then be getting recommendations from former students to others.

This is one business that requires patience and understanding, in addition to driving skill. If you are jittery about taking inexperienced drivers on the open road, get a partner who isn't, while you stick with the classroom instruction. This is a business which can easily provide a living for two or more individuals. In fact, you might find it advisable to set up your school so that women instructors teach women and men teach men. Establishing confidence in your students is the foundation of a successful course.

46 · Astrology Readings

Whether or not it is true that the Allies and the Axis powers used astrologers during World War II, the market for the so-called occult has gathered an ever-increasing number of believers from all age groups. Contrary to the opinion of many of the uninitiated, astrology is very distinct from palm reading and fortune telling. Smooth talk alone will not qualify you to become a successful astrologer. There are a huge number of texts and popular books on the subject, as well as dozens of syndicated newspaper columnists from around the nation, appealing to virtually millions of people. There has also been a very profitable market created by a company that sells astrology readings based on computer printouts. You send this company the exact date and time of your birth (along with a check for as much as $15) and you receive a highly detailed report back in the mail.

Astrology readers counsel their clients for a fee, usually from $10 on up. If you have an interest in this occult science, make an appointment with a "reader," then practice doing readings yourself on friends and relatives. You can find a reader in the Yellow Pages under "Astrology."

Once you have developed your own expertise in the practice of this occult science, put your own listing in the Yellow Pages. Aside from this expense, and perhaps a small classified ad in the newspaper, you will require no further investment. If you don't already have a mini-library of books on the subject, your local library should be able to provide you with enough reading matter to make you an expert.

For reasons that should be obvious, people love to have their horoscopes done, believers or not. It is a nearly irresistible temptation to get a glimpse of the future. And putting together people's personal horoscopes does not require an office or any elaborate, "mysterious" setting. Your home will do fine.

Once you have gotten experience with personal readings, it is really just a one-step extension to offer your horoscope service by mail, through the same kind of classified ad placed in your local newspaper as well as large papers from nearby cities.

With fees from personal readings, say of about one hour each, you could net several hundred dollars a week. By offering readings by mail, at least three or four typewritten pages in size, for a minimum of $15, your business could multiply geometrically. And you could easily find yourself in a position to hire a small staff and net yourself additional thousands of dollars.

Your customers, whether in person or by mail, are a prime audience for printed charts and books on the subject. The occult book market is strong enough to support publishing companies and retail stores that specialize in that subject, and make millions of dollars to boot.

With almost no investment you can augment your astrology reading business to include sales of printed material, birthstone jewelry, wall hangings and dozens of other items. With book publishers especially, you can order material, have thirty days to pay for it, and return unsold merchandise for credit. Write directly to the sales departments of publishers whose names appear in books on astrology.

All of the businesses mentioned here dealing with astrology—personal readings, horoscopes by mail and retail sales—can be run from your home, and should be, until your business warrants an additional expense for commercial space.

47 · Model Agency

Ask most people what they think modeling is all about and they'll tell you it's a glamour business where gorgeous girls get from $60 to $100 an hour. Don't you believe it. There is undoubtedly a tiny percentage of the business which features handsome young women and men in some of the nation's biggest magazines. And this elite group of beauties does indeed command rates from $60 an hour on up.

But 90 percent of the modeling business is devoted to supplying small advertisers, catalog publishers, department stores and clothing manufacturers with people of all types to model hats, jackets, bathing suits, gloves, rings and even exercise machinery. The rates per hour are more like $25 than $60, but this "second level" of the business provides most of the working models in this country. Very few clothing manufacturers are going to call Eileen Ford to send a high fashion model to show new spring wear to a group of out-of-town salesmen.

The whole point of this little exercise is to show you that you don't have to be a supplier of one-in-a-million faces to start your own modeling agency—and be very successful at it. Well, then, how do you get started?

Begin by assembling a stable of models. They all don't have to be young or beautiful (you'll get calls for character models of all types), but they do have to be photogenic. Run a classified ad that might read something like this: "Models of all types wanted. Experience helpful but not necessary. Must provide own portfolio. Send recent photo to ———."

Once you receive responses to your ad, and you should get many, you'll have to weed out the best and make appointments to see them personally. Those whom you want to sign to have you represent them exclusively will have to get together their own portfolio of several different shots showing their versatility. Arrange with a local commercial photographer to see these people. He may charge them for a shooting, or he may be willing to take their pictures for nothing to use for his own photographer's portfolio. Check with an existing model agency to see how they word their contracts and follow their lead. (Call one of these agencies as a prospective customer.)

After putting your group of models together, the other half of your business has to gel. That is, you have to line up clients. Although ad agencies are the largest users of models, they are by no means the only market. Manufacturers, mail-order catalog houses, retail stores and even local organizations sponsoring fashion shows all use models at some time or other. Put together a modest but tasteful circular, featuring your more attractive models, and send these announcements to as many of the above-mentioned markets as you can locate in your area. Better still, visit personally as many places as possible, and ask to see the art director, fashion coordinator, or whoever looks like they would be in charge of hiring your models.

Emphasize to your prospective customers, both in your circulars and advertising, as well as your Yellow Pages listing, that you offer immediate local service. This will be one distinct advantage you offer over the big-city agencies. When a prospective client asks to see a particular type of model you had better have a good supply of 8 x 10 glossies of each model on hand. These are not expensive to reproduce in sizable numbers (check with a commercial photo supply house for rates).

Rates for most models will be in the $25- to $40-an-hour range. All billing to the client is done by you. From your receipts you usually pay the model 80 percent of the monies you receive. You do not need commercial office space at the beginning since neither models nor clients have to come to see you (except for your first interview with prospective models). Your expenses will be for advertising materials, business cards, letterheads and telephone (plus answering service if you work alone).

In addition to the manufacturers, stores and agencies you contact, you would do well to visit every commercial photographer in your area and work as closely as possible with each one. Very frequently, these photographers get calls for work and are asked to supply models themselves. Become associated with them and they could provide as much as half of your business alone.

Obviously, the goal of your business is to keep as many models working at the same time as possible. With a good "stable," your 20-percent commissions can add up very quickly to net you literally hundreds of dollars a week, with almost no other expenses.

48 · Craft Instruction

If you do needlework, build model cars and airplanes, put up home preserves, or enjoy virtually any home craft, there's a vast market out there interested in learning the skills you may have been practicing for pleasure all these years.

If you've been practicing your craft in a basement workshop, your own kitchen or a sewing room upstairs, you have the basic space you'll need to give lessons. If you don't have the space in your home, you can arrange to use a student's house or even a rented hall at the "Y."

When you run a classified ad, and prepare 8½ x 11 brochures for your craft lessons, stress not only the pleasure to be gained from learning the craft, but the profit potential from turning that craft into sales of goods.

Here are some other advertising hints: If you do crewel work or embroidery, get the store where you buy your supplies to put your course announcement in a prominent place near their cash register. They'll not only be doing you a favor, but creating potential customers in everyone who has to buy thread, needles and other supplies to take your class. If you specialize in putting up home preserves, ask local fresh-fruit stands to tout your class on making jams and jellies to their customers. The point is to exploit positively *everyone* who benefits from the craft you enjoy—suppliers of raw materials, others whom you have taught your skill, friends and so on.

Begin by offering classes in early evenings or on weekends (this way you lessen your risk by keeping whatever day job you may have). For group classes of, say, up to five, charge from $1.50 to $2.50 per hour. If you are teaching photography developing and enlarging, for instance, and it takes a three-hour evening to conduct one class, make sure your rates cover you hourly. In other words, charge about $5 per student, plus costs for photographic paper, chemicals and any other necessary supplies.

As a supplement to income from a regular job, your craft-instruction classes can net you $100 or more each week. On a full-time basis you could double or triple that income.

In addition to teaching, create other ways to profit from your craft and contacts with your students. If you teach needlework, look into putting together preassembled kits to sell to members of your classes. If you teach pottery, hold showings of your students' work and offer the work for sale (with a commission to you on each sale). Start with classes, and once under way let your imagination lead you to ways in which you can parlay teaching into additional profit.

49 · Vanity Publishing

If everyone who wrote a manuscript had a publisher for his or her work, there would be hundreds of thousands of new books published each year (instead of the mere 40,000 new titles that flood the book market). The point is, there are many thousands of would-be writers around the country who would love to see their work in print, if only they could find an interested publisher. A substantial number of these "would-be's" not only have ready-to-print manuscripts, but money to invest in their work.

A vanity publisher, unlike more traditional publishing companies, gets paid by the writer to publish a limited number of copies of the work. At a prearranged cost per book, the vanity publisher takes a typewritten manuscript, may or may not edit this work, arranges to have type set professionally, then prints a specific number of copies which become the property of the writer of the work. The writer then seeks to sell or distribute copies of his own work, hopefully at a profit. The vanity publisher doesn't have to *hope* for a profit. It is already assured.

The first step in starting a vanity publishing enterprise is to advertise for original manuscripts. A small classified ad in *The Writer*, a magazine published in Arlington, Massachusetts, will draw a large number of replies. In your ad, call yourself a "private" or "cooperative" publisher, so as not to totally mislead readers into thinking you are a traditional publisher. Ask readers to submit original work along with a stamped, self-addressed return envelope. Once you have received a number of manuscripts, reply with a personal note outlining what it would cost the writer to publish 500 or 1000 copies of the work in hardcover.

To arrive at these costs (including your own profit) figure approximately $7 to $12 per page for typesetting (confirm these prices with a local type shop) and check with a small book printer to find out costs for printing. A small run of, say, 500 copies of a 100-page book could cost $2 or more per copy for printing and binding. Therefore, your cost for 500 copies of a 100-page book might be in the area of $2000. If these figures prove out in your area, you would charge your client about $6 a copy. You can suggest the client set a $9.95 list price for the book, which would give him or her a 40 percent profit if all copies are sold.

To people of means, $3000 is not an inordinate sum to invest in a manuscript they have produced. Your $1000 profit compensates you for your time and "production" work. Once into this business, you might be surprised to discover how many doctors, lawyers, business people and other professionals have a slim book of poetry or a novel hidden away, just waiting for a chance to be published. The gratification of seeing one's name in print, under the title of a book, is a strong motivation indeed, regardless of the real potential for retails sales of the book. One caution: Be sure you are paid in advance before committing money to publish a book.

50 · TV/Stereo Repair

With tens of millions of TV sets and even more stereo outfits owned in this country, it should be no surprise that the repair industry for these complicated electronic goods is a monumental business in itself. If there is one overriding complaint by TV and stereo owners it's the rip-off perpetrated by unscrupulous repair shops, replacing parts that aren't needed, using secondhand components instead of new ones (for which the customer is charged) and general lack of reliability.

If you have electronics training, you can start your own repair business with virtually no overhead. If you haven't been trained, there are two other options: a course in TV repair (offered by many private vocational schools or even by mail from someone like Heathkit) or partnership with a trained repair technician. Your repair business can be run from a basement or garage workshop. Pickups and deliveries can be made with a station wagon.

The stock-in-trade of a good repair service is, first, honesty and, second, reliability. Regional distribution centers for name-brand components will act as your parts warehouse, so you need invest no money for parts in advance. Tools and assorted nuts, bolts and small tubes are already assumed to be in your or your partner's possession. The only piece of equipment you may have to purchase is a tube tester. But until your business can afford this sophisticated piece of equipment, try to use a tester that belongs to the wholesale outlet from whom you buy parts. It may be an inconvenience, but well worth the initial savings when you are struggling to put together a business.

Advertise your service in the classified section of the newspaper as well as in the Yellow Pages. (Here is another case for using lots of "A's" in your service company's name to get a front alphabetical listing in the Yellow Pages.) And stress in your ads something unique in your service, such as, "Written Guarantee . . . Most Repairs Completed In Your Home . . . Free Pickup And Delivery When Necessary . . . Service Available Evenings And Weekends At No Extra Charge."

In addition to acquiring customers through direct advertisements, solicit appliance stores for service contracts. For a slightly lower fee, you then act as the store's service department, fulfilling guarantees on new equipment sold by the store.

Your rates to private customers should be based on prevailing rates in your community. A current average in many areas is $15 for a housecall. If the repair can be made in an hour or less, your fee will be $15, plus parts. You can mark parts up an average of 50 percent. If you have to remove a TV or stereo to your shop, the housecall charge of $15 will cover this cost. For in-shop repair work you should charge on the basis of $10 an hour. Remember, this is highly skilled work for which you or your partner have spent much time training. If you gain a reputation for honesty and reliability, your satisfied customers will use you again and recommend you to friends. You can net from $200 a week on up and be assured of continued goodwill from clients.

51 · Merchant Delivery Service

In every community there are drugstores, small department stores, gift boutiques, stationery shops, commercial printers and others who have to deliver packages to their customers Many of these sellers of merchandise do not have to make enough deliveries to warrant supporting a full-time staff person and vehicle. Combine service to several merchants in one delivery service and you have the makings of a profitable business with good growth potential.

To start this business you must have a small van. It need not be new, but it must be clean and fresh-looking since the van will be representing each of your client-merchants to the public. If you don't own a van, you could trade in your automobile and have the van double as a family car, at least at the beginning.

Advertising through the traditional outlets of classifieds and Yellow Pages is not the most effective way to get clients in this business. Remember your service is for retailers and others who deal with the public. Spend the small amount of start-up capital you need on business cards and brochures which should be delivered by *hand* to every merchant you can solicit. Talk to store owners personally. Impress upon them that they can save money by using your service for the hour or two of deliveries they may have each day or each week. With pharmacies, for instance, you could offer an emergency delivery service for prescriptions. With small commercial printers, offer deliveries on single boxes of invitations, which the printer could not afford to do otherwise. Stress that for the small service fee you charge, the merchant can offer a valuable additional service to his or her own customers.

The trick to success in this business, especially at the beginning, is scheduling. Of course you'll have to leave room for special unscheduled delivery service (particularly with emergency prescription-filling). But otherwise, you should arrange with clients to make pickups at their places of business on a regular basis. Within a short time you should know the streets of your community as well as a taxi driver, and therein will lie your ability to lay out delivery routes quickly and efficiently.

Your pricing can be based on two methods. One, a per delivery price for those stores that have no regular need for the service; say, $2 for each delivery. The other, a delivery contract to handle up to an agreed-upon number of deliveries each week. Before coming to a written agreement with a merchant looking for contract service, calculate carefully how much time and how many miles will be covered with an *average* delivery in town. Whether you drive or you hire a driver, figure $2.50 an hour for a driver's time plus 15¢ to 20¢ a mile for fuel and maintenance of your vehicle. These are your *costs* only. Add another 50 percent of that figure to take care of your net profit.

United Parcel Service has become an extremely successful nationwide service for the delivery of small packages. That company filled a need for intercity and interstate delivery. You can fill the local need for the same kind of service. Depending on the size of your community and your willingness, once successful, to branch out to neighboring towns and cities, you can enjoy similar individual success. Once you find yourself in a position to hire others to drive your vehicles, you must obtain bonding—a small but vital detail when you employ people to handle quantities of goods in a service capacity.

52 · Photographer's Representative

Commercial photographers, unless they are one of the few giants in the business, usually work alone, except for a darkroom assistant or a temporary helper on the job. We're talking here of the photographers who do shootings for advertising agencies, cosmetic companies and the like, as well as portrait photography. No matter how long a photographer has been in business, there is always a need to acquire more clients as well as service clients of long standing.

A specialized business in which you can learn the ropes quickly, and start with little experience, is "photographer's rep." This involves taking the professional photographer's work around to art directors, manufacturers, record companies (looking for album-jacket pictures) and anyone else who will possibly buy commercial photographs.

Because most one-person commercial photo studios require that the photographer spend as much time working as he or she can, there is little time to carry around a sizable portfolio to show to prospective clients.

The first step, of course, is to approach one, two, even several professional photographers in your community with a proposal to represent them to prospective clients in exchange for a commission on the work you bring in. Assuming you appear bright and reasonably knowledgeable, there is not a great risk on the part of the photographer. He or she puts together a very specific portfolio, sometimes geared to sell one job to a particular client, and you get paid only on those jobs you have arranged and sold.

There are two kinds of representation you can make. One is to professional clients like art directors at ad agencies, corporations putting together annual reports (which are always handsomely illustrated), jewelry manufacturers and anyone else in a position to pay for top-rate commercial work. The other market is professional portrait work. This can mean direct selling to the public by means of home visits, or possibly even setting up a temporary booth in a corner of a department store or lobby of a shopping mall.

Getting photographers to represent will be the easier half of the job. Place a classified ad stating, "Photographer's Representative Has Openings For A Few Good Professionals. Fee Arrangements Or Commissions." Visit the professional photographers who respond to your ad. Look carefully through their work and, for those whom you'd like to represent, decide on a trial period to see how the arrangement works. Then set up appointments for yourself with prospective buyers of the photographer's work. Instead of carrying around complete portfolios of several professionals' work, put together one portfolio of your own that carries a representation of two, three or four photographers' best work. Be sure to include tear sheets from magazines, catalogs and other printed pieces which show your photographers' pictures have appeared in publications.

When selling a portrait photographer's work to people in their homes, it is best to represent one professional at a time.

Your commission should be 10 percent of the photographer's fee. If the photographer wants you to assist on the job, this will cost more, and you should be compensated by the hour. But you'll have to play it by ear. If your photographer gets a $5000 job and asks that you spend two or three hours on location (nearby), it's obviously worth your commission to put in this little extra time gratis. If, on the other hand, a portrait photographer wants you to spend a day helping shoot a family of six in the studio, you should ask for additional compensation of at least $3 to $5 per hour.

Your investment to start this business should be limited to a small sum for advertising (to reach photographers), a desk and a telephone (right from your home). One person can represent as many as ten to twenty photographers without much assistance. Lining up three or four jobs a week can mean a commission income to you of as much as $150 or more. Once you have been in this business for a while, you'll discover that the clients you visited weeks ago may suddenly have a need for your photographer's work, in which case you are compensated for work already done (on your part). Be sure to leave business cards on all your calls, and follow up personal visits with telephone calls at frequent intervals.

53 · Floor Refinishing

Floor work, to a degree, is specialized work and can be extremely profitable. Let's start.

The basic equipment you need for this aspect of the floor business is a professional disc sander and a smaller sander called an edger. You can buy both of these machines for less than $300, but if that cash is unavailable right now, you can rent the same machinery on a daily basis from a rental outlet. The rental charge is usually about $15 per day plus sanding discs.

To get floor refinishing work, you advertise under "Miscellaneous Services" in the classified section of the newspaper, as well as take a listing in the Yellow Pages. This business will require you to give an estimate to your customers before starting a job, and hopefully you'll put your estimate in writing (and advertise that fact).

Refinishing a wood floor means sanding down the old surface, possibly staining the sanded floor, then coating the floor with varnish or a polyurethane protective coating. If you rent your sander and buy your stain and coating, you should be able to start the equivalent of three 10 x 15 foot rooms in one day. This means sanding, staining if necessary, and applying one or two coats of protective coating. You'll have to go back a second day to complete the protective coating work, but you won't need the sander.

Your cost for materials, including a rented set of sanders and discs, should be: $15 rent, $2 sanding discs, $12 stain and coating, and two men (yourself included) doing a day and a half's work @ $3 an hour—for a total cost of just over $100 for three 10 x 15 foot rooms. For a job this size, you should give your customer an estimate of $250.

Floor refinishing is very dusty work, and this should be clearly understood by your customer. Furniture should be removed from the rooms, and you should hang cloth in the doorways to prevent the sanding dust from spreading all over the house. Before a job is begun, make it understood that occupants of the house cannot use the floor for at least twenty-four hours, to give the coating a chance to set.

While working the job, be sure to clean every inch of the room after sanding but before staining or finishing. And this cleaning includes walls and ceilings which will undoubtedly have been coated thoroughly with a discernible layer of fine dust. An industrial vacuum would be a big help in this meticulous cleaning, but a broom and cloths will do.

You don't need a vehicle larger than a station wagon to transport your machinery. You should have an answering service, if you are working jobs yourself (which you certainly should do at the beginning). For assistance on the job, and most are two-man jobs, hire a part-time helper. One person handles the large sander and the other person works the edger. A minimum amount of skill is needed to run a sander, and this should come quickly from your first experience. Practice at home first, on your own floor if possible.

54 · Printing Broker

To the public at large, there is no such thing as a printing broker. There are just printers. The reason is that as a broker you are in essence a printer who jobs all his work out to other printers who happen to have press equipment. As a printing broker, you sell and service your clients, pick up the material to be printed and make sure it gets delivered, as well as collect for the job.

You call yourself "Jones Press" or any other name a printer might select, you advertise in classified sections of newspapers (if you deal with consumers directly) and you take a listing in the Yellow Pages, showing your home address and telephone number which is your "office."

Set up your business by first becoming associated with several print shops in your area. See printers who have different kinds of equipment that can be used to service jobs as small as 200 wedding invitations, engraved, and as large as 200,000 circulars to be mailed by a large department store or mail order house. Once you are satisfied that you know enough printers, with enough of a variety of presses, you are ready to solicit clients.

Your customers will be as widely varied as there are different printing needs, both private and commercial. You can sell personalized, printed Christmas cards, stationery, printed résumés, personalized notepaper, business cards and memo pads to individuals and companies. You also sell larger commercial jobs, like big-run circulars, brochures (one-, two- and four-color), annual reports, business forms and accounting sheets to your business accounts.

Although you will have the capability to provide virtually anything printed on paper, you'll find it's easier to succeed at this business by starting in one area, probably short-run jobs requiring less press sophistication than the big runs that get into the hundreds of thousands of one piece.

The only difference between you, as a printing broker, and an actual press shop owner is that you have the flexibility to use whatever press equipment suits your client's needs, while the press owner must first find work for his own equipment. Being in this flexible position means you can frequently come in with a better price for a job than someone who owns his own equipment, despite the fact that you are adding a commission on to your prices (as your fee).

Your stock in trade is, of course, good service. Visit all potential clients personally and bring work from the various printers you are associated with. The key to success in this work is bidding right for a job. When you have the opportunity to bid, shop around for the commercial printer who can give you the best price, efficiently. Associate with printers who will do the following: Give you a discount for regular work and deliver on time. There is no quicker way to alienate a client than to be late. Take your price from the printer and add 10 percent to 20 percent as your fee. Give your client only one price (never mention your "commission," your customer looks at *you* as the printer), and spend your time making sure the material is printed and delivered as promised.

With a growing list of satisfied customers, you can quickly find yourself in a very lucrative business, netting several hundred dollars a week. If you're a good salesperson, you have the basic tool for success. Watch your printers carefully, check frequently (at the printer's shop) on the progress of your jobs, and take nothing for granted. As with most service businesses, a good reputation among clients will be your best, most effective advertising.

55 · Weight-Loss Classes

Jean Neiditch, of Weight Watchers, Inc., was one of the earliest and most successful practitioners in an industry that has literally swept diet-conscious America off its feet. Her start in this business was simple enough: She took a good, common-sense diet (originally prepared free by the New York City Health Department), lost a sizable amount of weight, and began telling others of her weight-loss success. She realized that groups of people with the same problem could actually help each other work through the struggle to lose weight by mutual encouragement, peer pressure and supportive understanding.

From her modest beginning, Ms. Neiditch saw her Weight Watcher classes grow from a community influence to become a national franchise, and then on to prepared diet foods, sold in supermarkets, books on the subject, and literally thousands of deliriously happy "losers" around the world. But the basis of her success stayed the same: small groups meeting in a convenient place, led by average people who were successful in losing unwanted pounds, setting the example for others.

You don't have to aspire to corporate gigantism to become locally successful in your own weight-loss classes. The basic prerequisite, of course, is that you have to have lost weight, and you have to maintain your new weight. If you fit that qualification, you can tell others how you did it, and encourage them to do the same.

Your investment to start your own weight-loss class is minuscule. You should have a sound, approved diet to start with. (You might clear the diet with your doctor, just to be safe.) You then advertise for your first class, which can be held in your home, a neighbor's home, or even a meeting hall at a church or "Y." You must feel comfortable speaking before a group of people (you can practice by talking before family and friends first), and you must have a good scale at the meeting place.

Overweight people who come to meetings (held once a week) pay from $2 to $3 each time. The first thing is to weigh everyone and note their starting weight in a record book, along with the date. You then deliver your encouraging talk, showing pictures of yourself before you lost weight. Hand out mimeographed copies of your approved diet, and encourage the participants to put the plan into effect and come back the next week to check progress.

Subsequent to the success of Weight Watchers, there have been literally dozens of groups that have blossomed around the country using the same methods. Overweight people find it easy to identify with other working Americans who have overcome a weight problem, and they draw encouragement from becoming part of a group whose goals are the same.

Your income from this kind of business can grow very quickly. Twenty members paying $2.50 a class is just the beginning, and success in a few short months is not beyond reach.

56 · Custom Craft Sales

The craft and custom jewelry business is usually limited to the output of one person, but the profit margin is substantial on every item you sell. Crafts particularly have grown in popularity in recent years and provide a better-than-average living wage for a great number of people.

If you have ever created stained glass, needlework, tooled leather, silverwork, beads, macrame, candles, necklaces, bracelets, rings, settings, goldwork or any of a dozen other craft specialties, you have the potential for a successful business with little overhead. Your time and creative energy are your most valuable commodities. With crafts you may spend $10 on materials and sell the item you create for as much as $50, $75 or $100 or more.

The outlets for craft art have grown remarkably in recent years. Look in any newspaper and you will be likely to see an announcement for a craft fair taking place in a shopping mall, a public building, even galleries formerly reserved only for more traditional art.

To bring your craft to fruition as a business, you must first create enough pieces to be able to give a rounded showing of your work. Before your first excursion out of your studio, have at least six, ten or a dozen pieces of the craft you specialize in. Take a selection of your work to outlets like boutiques, men's and women's shops, gift stores, stationery shops. Specialty merchants frequently like to have available a certain number of related craft items which can either be sold right off the shelf or custom ordered.

Let's say that you are a candlemaker; you would take a carton of candles, say as many as twelve or fifteen different ones, to the outlets mentioned above. Offer to leave one or two pieces as display items which can either be sold or used as samples to order from. If materials for a candle cost you $1 and you have spent two hours making an individual candle, you could get as much as $10 for your candle.

You will have to price your goods competitively. The best way to see what the competition is doing, of course, is to visit other shops. In many cities you'll frequently find shops specializing in one craft only.

Figure your pricing on the basis of the cost of your materials plus $3 to $5 per hour for your time. Because it is the product of one person's efforts, the craft business is not one in which you grow rich quickly. But if you have always wanted to be compensated for your artistic labor this is a perfect opportunity.

In addition to offering consignment opportunities to local merchants, place a small classified ad in the local paper to solicit orders directly. You can work out of your home, assuming that is where you already have your craft shop. If you cannot attend to the phone at all the times, hire an answering service. Keep your expenses as low as possible, especially so-called overhead. Invite clients to your home studio or workshop to see goods for themselves. People will not expect a formal retail setting.

Check your community for others who produce different kinds of crafts. Groups of crafts people will frequently get together to have joint shows, sharing expenses. You might also look into art galleries in your area to see if they are handling crafts. More and more galleries are ready to consider crafts as legitimate art and are selling to people who only a few years ago would not have considered anything but painting and sculpture as true art.

Your profit potential in this business is good, but as with most artists, you probably won't become an instant millionaire. Many crafts people have become extremely successful. If your work is good, it could be in demand over a much wider area than your local community. Traveling to other communities to participate in craft shows could be very worthwhile. One day's sales alone can net several hundred dollars. Remember, you have to produce an output of work that merits a complete display, usually a minimum of five pieces depending on the size and complexity of your work. To become successful in this business you must be willing to tout yourself. Take your wares around and show them. Exploit every opportunity to gain exposure for your craft.

57 · Employment Agency

This is a business in which the size of your company will rarely be as important as the energy you put into the service you perform. When an employer is looking for the right person for the job, he or she doesn't care whether a small, one-person company provides that employee or a nationwide chain of agencies.

There are two kinds of advertising you must do. The first is to acquire a list of client companies which have a regular need for new employees. You should specialize. You might concentrate on secretarial help or other office personnel considered middle- or low-level management. Or you could specialize in higher salaried jobs, such as managers and others earning over $15,000 a year. Visit personnel offices of corporations in your area. Offer to send them screened applicants and encourage them to use your service as frequently as possible. If you become adept at locating and supplying a company with good people, you will obviously be called on frequently to fill other employment needs.

It's best to specialize in a *type* of employee, such as office help or sales help, or you can service particular industries, like publishing, advertising and other specific businesses. If you spread yourself out too thin you will have difficulty establishing service to a particular business.

After you have lined up a number of companies that will be interested in seeing screened applicants, the next course is to find applicants for those jobs. Run your classified ad campaign as if you were a large company. The point is, if you run a long ad (which may cost as much as $25 or $50) listing a number of specific job opportunities you will appear to be as large a company as anyone else who runs a sizable ad, regardless of the size of your office.

Start from your home to keep your expenses as low as possible. If you have a finished basement, or any room that offers privacy, you can set up an office to interview potential applicants for jobs. When you are soliciting for applicants, don't stop with classified ads. Contact local schools and colleges and get them to send their new graduates to you for interviews. The same methods should be used to sign up client companies. In addition to visiting personnel offices, send periodic mailings outlining the qualifications of applicants you have screened. Your mailings can be simple 8½ x 11 letters typewritten, then mimeographed. The letter should be addressed to the personnel director of a particular company. Stress the number of jobs you have filled, the kind of clients you service and, if possible, other companies that have used your service.

One other selling point to prospective client companies: Explain that you will advertise specifically for any job they want filled. Not only will you be helping them find applicants for the position, but you cost the client company less because you do their advertising for them.

Your fee, and how you get it, will depend on two things: the kinds of jobs you are filling, and the usual practices in your area. For lower paying jobs (salary less than $10,000 per year) the fee is usually paid by the applicant when he or she gets the job. Fees can range from one-third to one-fifth of the first month's salary. When an applicant comes to you for an interview, the first thing you should do is have the applicant sign an agreement that spells out the exact nature of the fee, who's expected to pay, and on what terms the fee will be paid. Usually an employee pays you a portion of each week's salary, if the employee is paying the fee. If the job only lasts for one or two weeks then you have gotten the fee that covers the amount of time the person worked. Sometimes employees just don't work out, even after they have been screened, interviewed and hired. This is one of the risks in this business.

If your employment agency specializes in higher paying jobs, it is not unusual for a client company to pay the fee. In this case the fee is usually 8 to 12 percent of a year's salary. This means that for a $12,000 job the fee can be as high as $1000. The best way to see how employment agencies in your area work is to visit them as a prospective job applicant. Look carefully at the form you have to sign, note how the interviews are done, discover who pays fees and under what conditions.

For those who have been in the employment agency business for a while there is the possibility of growing from what is called an employment agency to what is called an executive search firm. This is a highly sophisticated aspect of the employment agency business in which large corporations hire a consultant to find one particular person for an important job. You might, for instance, be given the assignment to find an advertising director for a large manufacturer. This requires confidential contacts with potential applicants, most of whom will already be working for somebody else. Delicacy, experience and tact are called for. This is one of the highest paying specialties in the employment agency business.

With an even moderate degree of success you can net as much as $25,000 to $35,000 your first year alone. The key to success is to place as many people as possible and to screen them properly so that a high percentage of the applicants you place stay with their firms. There is no higher recommendation than to have placed several employees who have worked out very well and have made the company happy.

Be sure to organize your files properly to keep track of the applicants who come to you for interviews. Make specific notes about their job capabilities and your rating of their abilities, based on an interview and the application. Stay with one field and you will have an easier time being considered a specialist. Keep your expenses low, start at home and work as a one-person operation until you have established yourself and have the money to hire office staff.

58 · Portrait Photography

Despite the fact that this country is flooded with inexpensive camera equipment and film processing, when people want a lasting photographic memento they do not rely on their own picture-taking ability. There is indeed a good degree of skill that goes into portrait photography. With practice, however, and a basic supply of lenses, lights and a good studio camera, you can become skillful in a reasonable amount of time if you aren't already.

Your expenses to start a portrait business begin with a good studio camera. This will require your largest outlay of cash and it can amount to as much as several hundred dollars. If you own a camera now that is something better than an Instamatic, you may be able to begin without buying a specific studio outfit. The other supplies you will need include lights and one or two reflector screens.

If you have to buy any equipment, consider starting with secondhand material. Photographic equipment doesn't wear out and you can often get serviceable used cameras and other supplies at less than half price.

Of course, you need not limit yourself to working in a studio. Many successful portrait photographers work outdoors in natural wooded settings. For many types of photos, this will give you the variety to enhance your appeal as a skilled portrait photographer. Parents often prefer to see portrait-quality photographs of their children near waterfalls and other natural settings.

Start by advertising as a portrait photographer in both the classified section of newspapers and the Yellow Pages of the telephone directory. Until you have an established list of clients, consider taking photographs of your own family or others to put together a portfolio. Work in both color and black-and-white. Have the photographs blown up to at least 8 x 10 or 11 x 14 size. Take, say, the six best portraits you have created and have five to ten enlargements of each made.

Visit merchants in your area, including camera stores, gift shops, clothing stores and children's shops, and ask if you can use a small part of the wall space to display your photographs. (Many shop owners will be glad to accommodate you. It offers a way they can decorate empty wall space and increases the service they offer their customers.) Make sure that near your display of photographs you have a 4 x 6 card with your name and telephone number.

Begin your business as an evening and weekend affair. Visit potential customers and schedule sittings and shootings at those times. If you're working in a studio it will not make any difference if it's in the evening, since you will be using artificial light anyway. If you are shooting in an outdoor setting, weekends may even be more convenient than weekdays.

Your market includes parents who want portraits of their children, family portraits, high school and college graduation portraits, bar mitzvah and wedding portraits, even publicity photos and pictures of executives for annual reports. You will be a specialist in photographing *people*, and there are obviously dozens of situations for which a person wants an elegant photo of himself or herself.

If you can, develop and print your own black-and-white photographs (you should of course be working in both color and black-and-white). By acquiring a secondhand enlarger, as well as skill in using this equipment, you will be able to produce black-and-white photos at a substantially lower cost than a commercial printer of negatives. For color work use a commercial photo house which will give you professional rates.

In addition to advertising in the newspaper and Yellow Pages, and through displays at various stores, you should personally contact corporations who need photos for annual reports, churches and synagogues who may want to recommend you to youngsters having communions and bar mitzvahs, even caterers who service weddings, engagement parties and other affairs. You can also consider hiring a photographer's representative whom you pay a commission based on business the representative gets for you (usually 10 percent of your fee).

Your fees, whether black-and-white or color, should be on a per-photo basis. If a client wants one 11 x 14, it is one price; 8 x 10s are another price; and a set of contact prints from the whole roll of film you shoot (approximately 3 x 5 or smaller) is another price. Large color mountings of 11 x 14 can sell individually for as much as $60 to $70 each. Some photographers charge for a sitting, plus a specific rate for each photograph. (This is to protect the photographer if the client wants *no* pictures after proofs are prepared.)

You should check portrait photographers in your area (as a prospective client) and see what the prevailing rates are in the community. You obviously have to be competitive.

In addition to the actual photographic work you can supply frames by making arrangements with a local frame maker and acting as his agent; you provide your client with a completely framed photograph at a prearranged rate. In this way you can make a profit from the frame as well as your photography.

Another outlet for your work: Submit particularly good photos to magazines for sale. Your client will get a model fee (not more than $25) for the use of this photograph. It is an attractive way for your clients to get paid while you make money on the published photographs as well. If you submit photographs for sale to a magazine be sure to include a self-addressed return envelope, as well as cardboard stiffeners to protect your photos. This is the only way you will get the pictures back when they are not used by the magazines.

A good portrait photographer can make upward of $25,000 a year. And you don't actually have to have that many clients to do well. One client who buys several enlargements of color photographs can net you as much as $150 to $200 alone. And that is after your expenses for processing, etc.

The key to success is to increase your photographic skill by practice and more practice. Take enough exposures at one sitting so that you have a good number of pictures to choose from for the single photograph that will be used as the portrait. Every good portrait you do is an advertisement for your work. Be sure to sign your name tastefully in a lower corner of the photograph. Recommendations will come from all your satisfied customers to their friends and relatives. Everyone is proud of a handsome portrait and the photographer is usually given the credit for making subjects look good in pictures.

59 · Pet-Boarding Kennel

There is a basic prerequisite for this business: You must have a reasonably good-sized piece of property on which you can allow pets running space. If you don't have property yourself, or don't have property large enough, you could consider renting a vacant lot on which you can construct fencing to make a runway.

You will have to construct at least one long, narrow area, approximately 25 feet by 6 feet, in which pets can get proper exercise. You should have some kind of heated building, possibly your garage, to take care of pets in the wintertime. Costs to build a kennel can be under $200 if you can do the simple construction yourself. Visit a local boarding kennel to get an idea of the space needed by dogs, cats and other pets to move around. If space is at a great premium, you can, if you're willing to start this business modestly, have accommodations for as few as five or ten pets in your own home.

Advertise your service both in the classified section of the newspaper under "Pet Care" and in the Yellow Pages. This is another instance where your company name with several "A's" at the beginning can get you business from people who call the first kennel they come to in the Yellow Pages. In addition to advertising you should make it a point to visit local pet shops and ask them to display a poster announcing your service. Also talk to dog breeders, who have a long list of customers, and to pet supply stores.

Once successful with a client you'll enjoy repeat business every time the customer goes away. Most boarding kennels get from $3 to $7 a day just for boarding. This means simply that the pet is exercised and fed. Charge additional fees for grooming services (which can increase your profit considerably). A shampoo alone, for a medium-sized dog, costs as much as $8 and need only take fifteen minutes. If you have the skill, offer hair-cutting services, tick and flea removal, and other pet care services which will making boarding pets in your kennel not only more profitable but more attractive to customers.

Although pet food, like everything else, has gone up in price, the cost for a day's pet food should be under 50¢ for a medium-sized dog, or any size cat. Depending on the competitive rates in kennels in your area, charge according to the size of the pet as well as the degree of care wanted by the customer. Very large dogs who eat two, three or four pounds of food a day will obviously cost you more to care for, and you should charge more.

Once you have constructed your runways and a heated area for the pets in cold weather, you have spent most of the start-up money you will require. You can net a good profit in a reasonably short period of time in this business. If your service is good you can make well over $10,000 a year. Of course, you must love pets to be successful. Not only because you will be dealing with animals on a daily basis but because your affection for pets will show very quickly to owners who come to you. There is really no better recommendation to a concerned pet owner than to feel that he or she is leaving a pet with someone who cares.

You should associate with at least one veterinarian in your area who can take care of any emergency that arises. You should also check into liability insurance, a natural precaution for this business.

Keep your accommodations clean and attractive. You will really be selling the pet owners rather than the pets, of course, and above all they want to make sure their animals will be well cared for.

This is a business which you can start and run by yourself, handling up to fifteen or twenty pets at one time. Any number larger than that will probably require part-time help in feeding and exercising.

60 · Advertisement and Publication Distribution

A weekly publication called *Penny Saver* was started in the Northeast recently. It is filled for the most part with advertisements from merchants in a single community as well as a few feature articles. The originators of this publication realized that in order to get the *Penny Saver* distributed quickly, on a weekly basis, they could not rely on the postal service because of the expense.

So this publication searched for an answer and found one. Each Sunday, a copy of the *Penny Saver* is hand-delivered next to each mailbox in a given area. The publishers found that it was both less expensive and more reliable to have their publication distributed by hand. And they are not the only ones who discovered the value of this specialized distribution service.

Many large stores who want to issue a sale catalog have found that hand distribution is a reliable and inexpensive way. Even smaller merchants found that a single sheet of advertising that they wished to publish could be distributed very effectively by hand in local communities.

The way the business works is this: Circulars or weekly newspapers are bundled in easily managed numbers and picked up by the chief distributor who then delivers the bundles to his employees. They in turn take a specific number of pieces and are assigned to particular neighborhoods.

This is a relatively new kind of service which has answered a need that the more conventional postal services did not seem to be able to fill satisfactorily. You can become a distributor of advertisements and publications with almost no investment at all. The first thing you should do is print a circular of your own to publicize your service. List a phone number at your home. You need not be concerned about having an elegant office, since you will be visiting clients outside your home. If you are engaged by a client who has a weekly publication to be delivered, you can establish your service on a contract basis and provide yourself with a regular income. You can also solicit department stores and smaller merchants offering your service on a one-time basis whenever the need arises.

You hire part-time help, such as high school students and others (with drivers' licenses if you live in a rural or suburban area). You pay your help approximately 1¢ for each circular or publication delivered, and you charge 2¢ to your customer. Although this may sound like small potatoes, you can easily service clients who publish as many as 30,000, 40,000 or 50,000 pieces each week.

You will have to organize local neighborhood routes (which you can do easily with the help of a street map of your community). Also visit advertising agencies in your area and tell them of your service. They may want to suggest this method of distribution to their clients.

Your stock-in-trade will be honesty of distribution. You have to be sure that the part-time help you hire is delivering the items conscientiously. One delivery person dumping a thousand pieces in a trash can can cost you a great deal. You do not have to do the actual delivery yourself, but you should certainly do one route to get an idea of how long it takes.

If you are not delivering yourself, make frequent spot-checks on your helpers to make sure that items are being delivered. Reminder: Circulars, newspapers, advertisements, publications, virtually anything being delivered by hand (that is, not by the post office) must not be put *in* a person's outside mailbox. You must place the advertisement or publication *next* to the mailbox. There is a postal regulation that prohibits putting anything except postal-delivered goods into an outdoor mailbox. Check your local post office for specific regulations regarding this kind of delivery. It's worth the effort and could save you aggravation, if not lost profit.

As your service grows and you acquire experience in making efficient deliveries, don't be surprised to discover you can make as much as $15 to $20 for every thousand pieces delivered—and that is net profit after you have paid your help. It won't take a mathematical wizard to figure out that 50,000 deliveries a week with a profit of $10 per thousand can net you a cool $500 a week for the equivalent of two or three days' work.

The most important point to remember is that you must be sure that your deliveries are made honestly. It will be definitely worth your while to make surprise inspections while your helpers are at work.

Once you have established your service, you can expand it widely, even to the point of delivering daily newspapers on a contract basis. Your rates should be figured on a per-thousand basis. You must have a good idea of how long it takes to deliver a thousand pieces, and the only good way to find out is to do it yourself, at least once or twice.

Because you can work deliveries one day a week, say a Saturday or Sunday, this is an excellent business to start in your spare time. Hold your day job without taking the risk of giving it up before you know whether you are going to be successful.

61 · Catering Service

Catering means literally what the word implies—"catering to other people's needs." People look for caterers for celebrations, weddings, bar mitzvahs, office parties, Christmas parties, virtually any occasion in which food is needed. But to start this kind of business you don't need anything more than a telephone and a desk in a room of your home, and a fair-sized kitchen in which you can produce sizable quantities of cold and hot food.

But food preparation is really just the beginning. As a caterer you can offer much more than food service. A catering service means sitting down with a client, working out the number of people who will be attending, and preparing the food that fits the client's budget. When figuring your basic food costs, calculate the costs of the ingredients, the time to prepare the food and serve it, as well as the salaries you must pay to part-time help.

Keep overhead to a minimum. Hire a staff only when you have a particular job to perform, so you do not have to pay people except when they are working.

In addition to catering to the food needs of your clients, you can offer complete services for any occasion. On Long Island, New York, two women started a catering service almost by accident. They started by helping a friend who was having a big party by preparing hors d'oeuvres and hot dishes. It was a successful party and they enjoyed the work, so they decided to offer a service to others in the area. Once, when they catered a wedding, they were asked to suggest a good dance band for the celebration, as well as a store where the bride and bridesmaids could purchase wedding dresses. This gave them an idea. After doing a little research they came back to the host and offered to cater the wedding from beginning to end, including bridal service, gowns for the maid of honor, dress clothing for the ushers, rings for the bride and groom, a musical group for the wedding celebration, and they even contracted for a hall where the celebration could be held. In other words they offered their client a complete service for a package fee. It left the parents of the bride free to attend to other matters, and after it was over they were so pleased they recommended the service to friends. These women became successful by extending their catering service to include every need for a given occasion.

You can get into this business without going to such lengths, but imagine how valuable your catering service would be if you could offer all these conveniences to your clients. It means, of course, that in addition to food wholesalers with whom you will deal, you must make arrangements with suppliers of paper goods, linens, decorations, jewelry, flowers, chairs and tables. To extend the service, for instance, to a complete wedding package, as these two successful women did, requires that you become familiar with one or more types of musical groups in the area, bridal salons that can provide formal clothing, jewelers who can supply rings and other small gifts to the wedding party, and even proprietors of halls for such an affair.

When you put together a package, whether it be something as complicated as a wedding or as simple as an office party, you must calculate your prices carefully up front. The host of the affair will be depending on your estimate, and you will be committed to putting together the party at the prearranged price.

Have the ability to work with different kinds of budgets. For instance, if a host wants to spend less than $5 per person you should be able to put together a variety of package offers. Your fees are based on a per-person rate and usually do not go below a certain minimum, such as $50 to $100 for your service.

Meet with your client in advance and carefully note every single element the host wants for the party, including types of food, amounts of money that can be spent per person, decorations, and anything else you will need to make this celebration a success. Once you have calculated your costs, as well as your time, add 25 to 50 percent above these costs as your profit. Don't forget that in addition to arranging for supplies, you will be required to attend the affair to oversee everything. You are, in a sense, the general of this campaign. You organize it, see that it runs properly and are prepared for any emergency that comes up, such as a spilled tray of food which you may have to replace quickly, or even a broken case of liquor which needs to be replenished.

If you organize well (and you can by writing everything down), you will be in control. With one or more successes under your belt you'll find that pleased customers will gladly recommend your service to others. And nothing will please a customer more than hearing compliments from guests as they are enjoying the occasion.

How much can you make? You can do extremely well, depending on how much time you are ready to give to this business. If it involves your full time and you have parties that you are catering to on, say, a once-a-week basis you could make as much as $20,000 a year or more clear profit. But you will work for this money, because your job is to do the *worrying* for the client as well as making sure everything runs smoothly.

You will be very successful if you make your clients feel that "there was nothing to it," that everything ran so smoothly that the hosts enjoyed the party as much as the guests.

When you contract with a host, and it should be a written contract, get an advance at the time the contract is signed. In this way you will be covered for initial outlays of cash. You should not have any overhead except a telephone at home, and perhaps a small advertisement in the Yellow Pages and classified section of the newspaper.

Most of your business should come from recommendations to others by satisfied clients. The profit potential is substantial if you are the kind of person who likes to attend to details and enjoys seeing an operation run smoothly.

62 · Nature School

Here is a unique business if you enjoy working with youngsters age eight to fifteen. It can be a bonanza in pleasure and profit. It's a school in which the "classroom" space is free, and almost all the supplies you need are there for the picking.

Glibness aside, if you like the outdoors and are in a situation which gives you afternoons, evenings and weekends to work, you can not only satisfy a desire to enjoy nature but you can impart that desire to others. The basic prerequisite is a knowledge of plants, animals, hiking and our natural environment. If you have not had deep experience in the area of nature you should at least have an abiding interest in discovering this exciting world. It doesn't make any difference if you are a city dweller or from a rural area.

Your nature school is a place where youngsters can go after their regular school day, as well as weekends and even full days during the summer. (If you happen to be a teacher this is a perfect business to tie in with your regular teaching hours.) The school is based on the idea that youngsters, wherever they live, have an interest in finding out about nature, have a desire to go on hikes (even during the fall and winter) and need adult guidance to educate and supervise them.

Start by advertising in the classified section of the newspaper. Post notices prominently on public and private school bulletin boards, at the local "Y" and other places where youngsters meet, including neighborhood variety stores. You would do best to limit the age group of the youngsters to eight to fifteen years old. If you can get enough students to form, say, two different groups, keep the age of the youngsters no more than two or three years apart. However, even a mix of children with six or seven years' difference in age can be exciting and rewarding.

In your announcements, stress that this nature school will emphasize a "learn by doing" process. You can take youngsters to wooded areas in your community on short hikes and teach them to identify different plants, trees and animal life. Demonstrate which wild plants are actually edible and how they can be prepared quite deliciously. There are several books on edible plants, the most famous of which is probably Euell Gibbon's *Stalking the Wild Asparagus.*

If you live in a city you can even use the public parks as your classroom. When the weather doesn't permit you to be outside, use a garage or even an apartment as a meeting place. As the founder and teacher of a nature school you will have to plan carefully. You must have enough activities planned to make a child's after-school hours pleasurable, exciting and informative.

Start with a ten-week school session, meeting twice a week for two hours each time. The success of your school will be based to some degree on the kinds of interesting activities you become involved in with your students. If you run your school alone, which you should at first, limit your enrollment to no more than ten to fifteen youngsters. Any more students in one class and you will probably need help in supervising. But let's say you have ten students and you charge $1.50 per hour, per student. This will net you $30 for a two-hour afternoon, $60 for two days of classes a week.

In addition to your classroom experiences with nature you can organize hikes, overnight trips and other "field" experiences that will add to a youngster's pleasure and awareness of outdoor life. This kind of after-school school will appeal particularly to families where both parents work. It will be an exciting opportunity for youngsters to enjoy themselves outdoors, learn to become more self-sufficient and at the same time remain under adult supervision.

Start your nature school from your own home. Avoid any expenses except your telephone and an occasional classified ad, plus, of course, a concerted personal effort to solicit the participation of schools and youth organizations.

You can adjust your "curriculum" to suit the seasons and the locale in which you live. During the summer, for instance, you can arrange and lead canoe trips, nature walks, backpacking tours, even horseback riding trips, all for a fee. During school vacations you can plan week-long trips to various places. It's important, of course, to have your plans well organized and to make sure that you have insurance (as you should any time you are performing a service in which you are responsible for people, particularly children).

If you can fill your classes with a minimum of ten students and run two or three different groups each week, you could easily net

$200 or more. Your cost for materials will be minimal as you can expect to find all your teaching tools available free in "nature's backyard."

You must enjoy working with children and you should obviously be someone who enjoys the outdoors. Learn detailed facts about plant life in your area, as well as outdoor living techniques and even water recreation. Books are available by the thousands in most libraries to give you as good an education as you will need to lead youngsters through nature effectively.

This is not a business that will make you a millionaire; it is a way to take pleasure in the outdoors, to give youngsters the pleasure of the same experience and make money at the same time. Of course you can parlay this activity into even higher profits by expanding your nature school into a summer camp. This, of course, means hiring a staff and requires a whole series of detailed plans and investments by itself. The simpler nature school is a business for someone who wants to enjoy an outdoor life, is satisfied with a moderate income and enjoys working with children.

63 · Calligraphy

The art of calligraphy (decorative, artistic handwriting) has been with us since the Middle Ages, when monks sat for years in tiny cells reproducing the Bible in exquisite handwritten letters. The art itself has been replaced in many cases by the printed message, which can virtually duplicate any type of written art form. However, those who want special invitations for important events, such as weddings, communions, bar mitzvahs and other momentous occasions, frequently want to have an even more memorable invitation prepared for guests at such affairs.

The job of a calligrapher who does custom invitation work is highly specialized. If you have an artistic hand you can learn different styles of decorative writing from illustrated books. Your basic tool is a pen, probably an italic fountain pen. You can buy such pens at most stationery stores and some even come with a book of instructions on how to create decorative handwriting. Your work is done on a per-piece basis. You'll usually be writing the name and address of the recipient of the invitation on an envelope, and perhaps a message or name on the invitation itself.

Your business should also offer a complete invitation preparation service to your clients. You design the invitation, have the engraving done by a printer, and then hand-letter the envelopes yourself.

Start by running classified ads in the newspapers and put a listing in the Yellow Pages under "Wedding Announcements." In addition to advertising, make contact with local caterers and arrange to service their clients (as well as pay the caterer a percentage for all business he or she brings to you). Check your newspaper for engagement announcements. These are usually placed far in advance of the wedding. Contact the bride's family directly and try for an opportunity to visit them in person. Explain that you would like to show some examples of your work as well as explain how your very attractive handwritten invitations can cost little, if any, more than mere printed invitations.

Associate with one or more printers who will give you discount rates on engraved invitations in return for the promise of repeat business on your part. When you visit a client make sure you have several samples of your work at hand. If you are just starting out, prepare three, four or five different kinds of handwritten invitations of your own design as your "portfolio."

Since invitations have to be addressed anyway, you can make a good case for taking that burden off the bride's family while they have so much else to be concerned with. And for just slightly more than it would cost for plain ballpoint pen handwriting on the envelope, you can make their invitations more elegant than they ever thought possible. If you have ever received a handwritten envelope done by a professional calligrapher, you will not soon forget how attractive this kind of work looks.

It will be your job not only to do the handwriting on the invitations but to design an invitation that will suit your client. Printers should be able to provide you with a style book that illustrates dozens of different kinds of invitations with a wide choice of type faces and themes. When you contract with your client to prepare a certain number of invitations, your price should be figured on a flat fee basis.

If you can address two invitations a minute (over 100 an hour) you can charge as much as $35 for 100 and come away with a good profit for your efforts. The printing charges would be about $10 to $15, which means that those 100 invitations net you up to $25.

You can clear as much as $150 a week or more by working alone. Hire part-time help, whom you can train to write with a decorative hand, and you can net several hundred dollars a week, even after paying staff salaries. You can hire people to work at home on a part-time basis and pay them on a per-piece basis. Some clients may even want a select number of invitations completely handwritten for a special affair. Figure your pricing on how much handwork is involved. If your part-time help costs 5¢ per invitation, in addition to printing, you can profit on both the printing and the handwork.

This business allows you to expand with very little risk, because you are utilizing help on a piecework basis. You pay only for work done, rather than for time involved. Learn several styles of handwriting, such as Old English, Gothic and other decorative styles that will give invitations a particularly rich appearance.

In addition to invitations, put your calligraphy talents to work by making attractive wall plaques by copying a recipe on a large 8 x 10 piece of colored card stock or bond paper. Then by laminating this card or paper to a board you can create a very attractive wall hanging for kitchens. Wall hangings that are handmade and custom-designed could sell for as much as $10 or more each. Materials should cost you no more than $1. You could also, for example, create custom-designed book stickers, scrolls for award presentations, hand-lettered testimonials or proclamations on parchmentlike paper, even diploma designs for small schools.

If your calligraphy talent can be used for craft creations, you should employ other methods to distribute your goods. In this case, make a point of having several decorative pieces available for consignment use by local gift shops, boutiques and stationery stores. Handmade, custom-designed items are in great demand, because even at prices like $10 or more they provide a work of original art to those who want to have unique but inexpensive decor in their homes.

Virtually anything that requires decorous handwriting can be enhanced by your service. You should get a minimum of $7 to $10 an hour for your specialized talent (though you should quote jobs on a per-piece basis).

64 · Garage Sale Organizer

One of the most popular ways people have to both sell and acquire secondhand goods is through garage sales, also called tag sales in many areas. It is a personal rummage sale by a homeowner who is either moving or just wants to sell a lot of used garden tools, furniture, appliances and other household items that the family may not have use for any longer. To put one of these sales together yourself is an arduous task. You need energy and good planning. This is difficult for older people, in particular, who cannot lift heavy loads.

In addition to preparing household goods for a garage sale, the selling itself requires a bevy of helpers. An answer to this problem, one that has become particularly profitable in recent years, is a business in which you run a garage sale for others. As a garage sale organizer you would be responsible for going to a person's home, looking over all the goods to be sold, pricing the goods and actually running the sale. You should have an awareness of what secondhand merchandise in each category is selling for.

As a garage sale organizer your emphasis should be on organization. You can run this business by yourself, but you should hire part-time help (preferably able-bodied students) to carry merchandise and set it up for display. A garage or tag sale takes place right on the property of the homeowner, with merchandise displayed in the the driveway, yard, garage or right in the home. You should start preparing for a tag sale with your customer at least a week in advance. This doesn't necessarily mean that you have to spend every day of the following week working on this particular sale, but you should allow yourself enough time to organize it properly.

The materials to run your business are really minimal. A phone number to begin with (right in your home), tags for marking prices, and that's about it. Advertise your service in the classified section of your newspaper.

You should have a good sense of what kind of merchandise sells best and, of course, how to price everything from secondhand hedge clippers to brass beds and used clothing. (You can get a quick education by spending a few hours on any given Saturday at a number of tag sales in your area.)

Make sure, when running your garage sale, that household goods to be sold are placed for easy viewing by you or your helpers. There is a problem, of course, watching out for people who go to tag sales to rip off small merchandise. Keep items like costume jewelry, dishes and glassware on a large table near the place where you are collecting money from customers who visit to buy.

Your fee as a sale organizer runs anywhere from 15 to 30 percent of the price paid for goods. You should have a notebook in which you record every piece of merchandise (preferably by category) with the retail price you are asking. When you have sold an item, you note it in a space provided in the notebook. Your client may be willing to bargain on many items, in which case the price you receive is less than the asking price.

Everything is ripe merchandise for tag sales. People have sold cars, motocycles, rider lawnmowers and other heavy machinery which bargain hunters are quick to snap up if the price is right.

Organizing and running a tag sale requires one or two days to set up the merchandise plus the days in which the sale will be running.

Much of the organizing work can be done in the evening. The running of the sale usually takes place on a Saturday and/or Sunday when business is most likely to be brisk.

How much can you make? For the equivalent of two to five days work you can walk away with a surprising sum of money. If your commission is 20 percent on all goods sold, you could easily clear $200 from one tag sale, depending on what kind of merchandise your customers have to sell.

Several garage sale organizers have expanded their business to the point of buying whole households full of furniture and other items. The sale organizer visits his or her customer and offers the option of either running a sale on a commission basis or buying the whole lot of goods for an agreed price. Obviously the price offered for a house full of goods is going to be low enough to allow substantial profit, just as if you were buying out a whole estate. In this case the garage sale organizer frequently works directly with an estate auctioneer who has facilities for storing large quantities of goods.

Part of your service requires that you run a classified advertisement for the garage sale. Depending on rates in your newspaper this will cost from $10 to $50 and should be taken into account when you calculate your commission. The point of your ad, obviously, is to draw as many people as possible to the sale. Therefore, make the ad as specific and detailed as possible. That way you are more likely to advertise at least one item that will appeal to a great number of people. Make your ad longer than most other garage sale ads to draw attention to the sale.

Your income from this business can grow quickly. It is not unusual for good organizers of garage sales to net several hundred dollars a week.

65 · Pottery Selling

Handmade pottery is one of the most attractive craft items sold. It doesn't take a great deal of skill to make simple pottery items like bowls and single plates with attractive designs. It does take practice, however, and dexterity in the use of a potter's wheel and you have to learn by trial and error how to "fire" your clay in a kiln. But even a beginning potter can create items that are extremely attractive and very salable.

If you're going to create and fire your own pottery, this business does require a small investment. A manually operated potter's wheel can be purchased for $50 to $60; a used wheel can be purchased for less but you will have to shop around. A kiln is a heavier investment but can bring you additional income from "renting" kiln time to other potters. Kilns cost several hundred dollars. If you're lucky enough to find a used one you might be able to pick it up for less than $200. They are priced according to size, and if you're going to have an income from renting space in your kiln to other potters you have to have one that is large enough to hold several items.

If you have a studio at home, either in a garage or basement shop, you have the space you need to both create and sell your pottery. If you do not have the facilities in your own house or apartment there are studios where you can rent both time and use of the kiln. In this case, of course, your cost for materials (including the money necessary to prepare and fire your pottery) will be more. But pottery, being as attractive as it is, can command a substantial mark-up above the cost of the materials. If, for instance, you spend $1.50 for a certain type of clay and it costs you another $2 to rent kiln time then you have basic material costs of $3.50. Yet you can ask, and receive, up to five times the actual cost of materials.

Pottery is an extremely rewarding hobby with few limitations on creativity. You can even create items like ashtrays, trays, wall plaques and figurines that can be prepared by the slab or pinch method, or in molds (in which case you have no need for a potter's wheel). Molded items are made simply by pouring a mixture into a form. They then harden and are baked in the kiln. ("Sign" your pieces with a stylus, and you have created an original piece of art in much less time than it would take to create, say, a complicated oil painting.)

Before trying to sell your pottery, create enough pieces to offer a good selection. You should start with a minimum of a dozen to thirty pieces of pottery, which could take you two weeks or more to prepare.

You can sell pottery in your own studio or you can join with other potters, perhaps even organizing an artists' co-op in which the work of several people is displayed in one place. This "place" could be someone's garage or home studio. As the organizer of an artists' co-op you would be entitled to a small commission (say, 10 percent) on the sale of other artists' work. In addition to selling pottery through your own retail outlet, take your goods to gift shops, boutiques and other fine stores. Offer the pottery on a consignment basis and let it be known that you will also take custom orders, even with decorating and design to the wishes of a particular client.

Unlike many other crafts arts, pottery is not only attractive but functional. Once you become adept you will be able to create a whole set of handmade dishes and other items which require substantial skill.

In addition to selling pottery, set up classes to teach your talent, especially if you have access to one or more potter's wheels and a good-sized kiln. Price your tuition for classes so that you are compensated for the use of materials. Make sure that you calculate not only the cost of clay but the electricity to run the kiln. The kiln is simply a special oven that uses large amounts of fuel to build up very strong sustained heat.

With a combination of selling your pottery and teaching classes it is possible to net several hundred dollars a week. And this can all take place right in your home. (Be prepared to pay a high electric bill. A kiln can cost as much as $10 to run for just part of a day.)

If you've had little or no experience as a potter, enroll in a class yourself, or visit a potter's studio in your community. Try to use commercial suppliers of various types of clay, wheels and kilns, as opposed to retail hobby shops.

Advertise your pottery and your classes in the classified section of the newspaper and make sure that churches and organizations in your community receive announcements. Check trade journals to acquire used potter's wheels and kilns at substantially reduced prices. This is a hobby which you should enjoy first and foremost and secondly think of as a venture for profit.

66 · Welcoming Service for Newcomers

Most people who have ever moved into a new community have quickly become aware of such services as Welcome Wagon and New Neighbors. These organizations were set up initially to make the transition into a new community easy for people from out-of-town. It has turned into a very profitable venture because the welcoming service solicits different merchants in the area and, for a fee, hands out a packet of money-saving certificates that encourage the newcomer to shop at various stores in town.

Newcomers to your community will of course be delighted to be welcomed to town, especially if they have moved from far away. The added bonus of discount certificates from local merchants is gravy. Usually the fee to the merchant is based on a rate of 50¢ to $1 per brochure or discount certificate handed out. You can solicit every merchant in town, including food markets, gift shops, clothing stores, even the town newspaper. Your list of merchant-clients need be limited only by the number of people whom you approach. The price to the merchant is really quite small. The possibility of new, repeat customers is very alluring.

The first thing to do is acquire clients from among local merchants. You can even have the certificate or announcement printed for your merchant-client on a fee basis (in addition to rates you charge for handing out these circulars).

Once you have a good representation from merchants in the community you are ready to start business. If you have a station wagon, or even a family automobile, you have the transportation you need to get to newcomers' homes.

There are several ways to locate new arrivals. One is to keep in touch with the real estate community and make yourself aware of house sales transacted in your community. You can also gather information by checking the public notices that banks put in newspapers announcing mortgage arrangements. The idea is to get to know who will be moving into a new home well in advance of their arrival. To be effective you should visit new homeowners within four weeks of their arrival. Otherwise, you diminish the effect of the advertising you are going to be presenting. The newcomer will have already begun shopping and may or may not have visited stores other than your merchant-clients.

In addition to circulars and discount certificates from local merchants, offer new arrivals information about your town. In many communities organizations like the League of Women Voters publish a general information booklet about the town. Visit your local Chamber of Commerce. Their job, of course, is to provide a stimulus to business in the community and they frequently have substantial amounts of materials that they are usually more than happy to have distributed free.

As the owner of a welcome service you can earn $200 a week or more depending on the number of new families who move into your commnunity each year. This business is particularly good for suburban areas to which executives and others are constantly being transferred by large corporations.

The average homeowner in this country moves once every five years. This is a national average and may not apply to your area specifically, or there may be even more frequent moving in your community. The point is that if you visit, say, two homes a day, five days a week, you will spend from a half hour to an hour and a half talking to the new homeowner and presenting him or her with helpful information as well as money-saving announcements.

Educate yourself about the public services available in your community. In addition to representing merchants, you will in fact be representing the town.

If you are able to carry different announcements from merchants at a cost of 75¢ to the merchant you will be making $7.50 for each visit to a new home. This income will grow substantially when you can branch out and hire others to distribute certificates and information for you. Women looking for part-time work, who have children in school, are prime candidates as staff for a welcoming service. Usually they can make calls anytime up to 3:00 in the afternoon, before their children get home from school. The service can provide an excellent part-time income for them, and you need only pay your help on a per-visit basis.

Before committing yourself to any expenditure, spend some time at your town hall Check the statistics on how many new families move into town each month. The more you know about your town, including the number of new families you can reach, the easier time you will have selling merchants on the value of your service. You should be able to clear from $5 to $10 for each visit to a new arrival. At the beginning you may be willing to charge less for your service, to prove its value, but your income should grow to the point where, for working perhaps two hours a day, five days a week, you could make close to $100. Not a bad part-time income.

Organizations like Welcome Wagon have grown from a single-community effort to become a nationwide franchise. In addition to local merchants, Welcome Wagon staffers now distribute announcements from national organizations, especially sellers of mail-order products from book clubs, record clubs and the like. If you can offer a good guaranteed distribution, contact book clubs and record clubs by mail and offer to distribute their advertising material for a fee. It could be a good source of additional income, with little or no additional effort.

67 · Telephone Solicitor

The telephone, as a selling tool, has become more and more useful in recent years, especially as selling techniques have become more sophisticated. It is an ideal business for someone who wants to work from home, or who cannot travel easily. There is virtually no limit to the kinds of things that can be sold by telephone. Here is a partial list: newspaper and magazine subscriptions, roofing and home repair services, small merchandise like light bulbs and paper supplies, classified advertising, carpet and furniture cleaning, lawn care service, even real estate.

Most businesses that contract to have their goods or services sold by telephone pay a commission on a per-order basis or a per-inquiry basis. For instance, if a roofing contractor engages you to line up potential clients for his service, you will be paid just for getting the person you're calling to agree to see a representative from the roofing company. It's not difficult to see the value to a seller of a service to get a prescreened inquiry rather than simply wait for a response from some ad he may have run.

To get into this business you must first line up clients who want to have their goods or services sold by telephone. It can be done on a no-risk basis to your client because he pays only for those solicitations that pan out as inquiries or sales. But if a roofing contractor, for instance, is able to get a $500 job because you lined up a client by telephone, it is well worth his while to pay as much as $5 just to have the name of a potential customer. Of course, all you need to run your telephone soliciting service is the telephone itself. You need not leave your home to perform your service, so there is no need for an office or any other rented space. Once you have lined up one or more clients interested in paying a commission for your solicitation work you are ready to start.

Charge your clients on the basis of the amount of money they stand to make by having you sell their service. A roofing contractor with a potential $500 sale could be worth as much as $5 to $50 to you in commissions for each inquiry. Most of your telephone-sold goods and services will be in the $50 or less range, such as subscriptions and carpet-cleaning services.

(There is also a market for telephone survey work for opinion-poll companies. This is easier because you are not asking the person you reach on the phone for money, rather just for a few minutes of their time to answer some questions.)

The greatest difficulty in telephone solicitation is overcoming the initial resistance to the intrusion. You have to develop a technique for disarming people of their natural reluctance to talk to someone who wants to sell something.

Real estate firms, especially those dealing in vacation property, are one of the prime users of telephone solicitation. The purpose is not to sell a piece of real estate by telephone but simply to get the person to express an interest in receiving more information. Those who solicit business by telephone frequently have their own lists and simply need a sales-minded person to do their telephoning for them.

Telephone solicitation is a specialized talent that can be developed by practice. You can make hundreds of dollars a week, and as your technique improves so does your income. With the growth of your business you can hire others to work for you, paying them from the percentage you receive.

68 · Personal Investment Counseling

There is a special prerequisite for getting into this business. You have to have a familiarity with the major stock exchanges as well as experience in dealing with brokers.

If you do fulfill this requirement (or you have time to learn the business of investments) then you have the basic qualifications for becoming a personal investment counselor. Many middle income families, as well as more affluent ones, have money that they wish to invest to provide a greater return than savings banks. Personal investment counseling is very different from commercial brokerage work. You must be capable of looking at a family's financial situation to make recommendations that suit family needs now and for the future.

You must also familiarize yourself with life insurance plans and investments that are designed for individuals rather than corporations, such as mutual funds and personal acquisition of municipal bonds (tax free).

If you're an investor who wishes to leave the rat race of the big city, this business could provide you with a very lucrative income, as well as provide many families with a much needed service.

Advertise your service in the Yellow Pages under "Investment Counselor." But you will be more than just an investment advisor. You must be ready to evaluate the complete financial picture of a family. Many life insurance agents are adept at this service, having been trained by their parent companies. If you think this field of business may appeal to you but have little experience, you can get training as a salesman with a large insurance company. These companies provide their sales personnel with remarkably sophisticated tools for evaluating the financial condition of the family. The difference, of course, is that as a personal investment counselor you are serving only the family that you have as a client. An insurance salesperson is directing his clients so that they will buy from his insurance company. Insurance background can be very useful and can provide you with information that would otherwise be unavailable.

Consider each family that you advise as an individual "portfolio." Handle the family account as businesses handle their own accounts, with a clear picture of the financial input and the financial needs of that family unit.

It will be your job to discern the stated and unstated goals of the family you are counseling. But your counseling will not simply be to advise where to invest extra money. You will also be called upon to help a family plan its financial future in terms of anticipated earnings and anticipated obligations.

Your fees can be arrived at in two ways. You can take a percentage of the "portfolio" that you are managing, or you can charge an hourly consultation rate. Your fee, by the hour, should be from $15 to $40, depending on the sophistication of the advice you are called on to give (as well as the financial resources of the family you are advising).

You should become an expert on retirement planning, insurance needs and family budgeting.

To get clients for your business, advertise in the proverbial Yellow Pages and take an occasional classified ad in the newspaper. However, your greatest number of clients will come from personal referrals. Get to know local bankers who could recommend your service to their clients. People at banks and insurance companies in your community will be a prime source of clients, since they are in daily contact with people who have money needs.

This is a business in which you can devote as much or as little time as you choose. You should spend no more than one or two hours at a given consultation with a client. But your bill should also reflect the time you spend away from the client evaluating his or her financial needs. Like any professional, your bill will reflect a professional's hourly rate. You should also have an affiliation with a brokerage house.

As a full-time occupation, personal investment counseling can net you upward of $50,000 a year. This can also be a part-time occupation. For the few hours a week you spend you can make as much as $10,000 a year or more. This is a good business for a person who has had experience in finance and either wishes to devote time to other activities or wants to retire from full-time work. Your list of clients will grow as your service proves satisfactory. Although advertising will certainly not hurt, your business will come mostly from personal recommendations by members of the financial community, including banks and insurance companies as well as satisfied clients. Before starting this business you must register with the Securities and Exchange Commission. Simply write the Securities and Exchange Commission, Washington, D.C., and ask them for an application to become a personal investment advisor.

69 · Commercial Photography

Commercial photography is defined as any use of a camera to make money. And there are indeed many ways. You don't need expensive camera equipment to make picture-taking pay. Here are just some of the different areas in which commercial photographers have become extremely successful:

—Fashion photography for publications as well as manufacturers of clothing
—Real estate photography for agents and others who need pictures of land, property and homes
—Wedding photographs
—Bar mitzvah pictures
—Photo journalism
—Greeting card manufacturers
—Passport photographs

If you have a camera, and you enjoy taking pictures, there is definitely a market for your work. How skilled you become at taking a specific type of picture will determine, of course, your degree of success. You don't have to have years of training to get into this business.

You should have a reasonably good camera although you can start with a camera as modest as a $15 to $20 Instamatic. The idea is to choose your area of specialization first. Let's say, for instance, you have chosen to begin with real estate photography. In this case, first take several pictures of homes in your area showing the property attractively. Take your work to a few of the real estate agencies which proliferate in most American communities. Offer to take pictures of homes listed with the agency. The idea in real estate photography, of course, is to take pictures of homes in their most attractive light so that they will appeal to potential buyers. Practice shooting from different angles and at different times of the day. The pay for real estate is anywhere from $10 to $50 for a picture that the agency can use to print from. Get several agencies to call you whenever a photograph of a home is needed. You could find yourself earning several hundred dollars a week simply taking pictures of houses and industrial sites.

Let's say you want to become a photographer of weddings, bar mitzvahs and other celebrations. You are hired on a flat-fee basis, say $150 for a wedding. For this $150 you agree to provide a minimum of 20 black-and-white photographs of the affair which your client will choose from as many as 200 or more pictures you actually take. For color work, in which you will be required to have a little more sophisticated equipment such as floodlights and a good camera, you will be able to charge two or three times the amount you can charge for black-and-white work.

Regardless of what photographic specialty you choose, associate yourself with a commercial developing house which can provide you with enlargements at wholesale rates. Your fees for most types of photographic work will be either on a per picture or on a per job basis.

If you have photographs of outdoor scenes that would make attractive greeting cards, send a selection of these color photos (for which you should have original transparencies in your possession) to major greeting card printers. Send appropriate photos to record companies which are looking for illustrations for record jackets.

As you build a photo file you will find that an attractive commercial photograph might also serve as a possible landscape photograph of interest to a calendar printer. If you are taking candid pictures of people, whether or not they are aware of you taking photos, you must have releases from these people if there is any possibility that the picture will be published at some time in the future. A release form is simply permission in writing from the subject of the photograph to have that picture used for certain purposes. Write a release form yourself that simply says, "I [subject's name] give [your name] permission to use this picture of me for any purpose he sees fit."

Purchase several photography magazines to get an idea of additional marketplaces for your work (as well as hints on better photo techniques). This is a business which you can run from your home with no overhead except for film and developing. Solicit all types of clients and submit photos for publication regularly. Don't give up if you have submitted a dozen photos to a greeting card manufacturer or a publisher. With practice and good technique your photos will sell. There is an enormous market for photo work and you should not eliminate any possibility. Advertise your photographic work in the local newspaper, have business cards printed, list yourself in the Yellow Pages. Solicit commercial clients such as real estate agents, publishers of magazines, caterers who service weddings, and anyone else you can think of.

Your outlets for photographs are almost unlimited. You can send photographs to any publication as long as you enclose a stamped self-addressed envelope for the return of your pictures.

The income potential for a commercial photographer is substantial. It's hard work to get clients. It's frequently difficult to sell your work, but when you do, the rewards are substantial because the fees paid for photographs are far above both the material and time invested in it. It is an art form, and as you improve and persevere you will be rewarded accordingly.

70 · Library Research Service

Thanks to the proliferation of very well-stocked libraries in this country, there is practically no subject that cannot be written about extensively without ever leaving the confines of a library reading room. The call for research services is substantial—more than most people realize. If you were good at putting term papers together in school, or if you enjoy compiling information, this business can provide you with a good profit and virtually free access to millions of words on almost every subject imaginable.

Those who use research services include writers who have a need for documented facts in a given subject area, corporations that want material on specific subjects, academic people who want information in a particular area of study but do not have time to do the research, government agencies putting reports together on various subjects, even college students who wish to pay for the service of acquiring data for a particular classroom assignment. Most research services are limited to the humanities. And unless you have a particularly sophisticated knowledge of mathematics or a branch of science, your research will be most used by people needing general information, biographical data, historical facts and literary information.

Several years ago, two students from Massachusetts started a highly profitable business by providing "research material" to college students and teachers from around the country. The student or teacher would write to this service asking for a specific number of typewritten pages on any of literally thousands of topics, from a survey of the work of Charles Dickens to an economic treatise on the Depression of the Thirties.

You do not have to be an expert in the subject matter you have to research. The information is freely available in most libraries, and your job as a researcher is to know where to look rather than to be an independent well-spring of knowledge. If you know how to use the card catalog of a public library and can understand the simple filing methods of the Dewey Decimal System, you have the basic tools to begin your business.

To acquire clients for a library research service you begin by advertising in college newspapers, as well as placing announcements in schools and even libraries (wherever you can get permission). You can also advertise in national magazines and newspapers with ads costing as little as $20. Get a copy of publications like *The New York Times Book Review*, various literary magazines, *Saturday Review/World* magazine and college publications from around the country. (You can even go to the library to find samples of most of these publications.)

Charge for your service by the number of double-spaced typewritten pages you are asked to produce on a given subject. Of course, the more difficult the research the more expensive your service (and the more time it will take), but unless you have to make a special trip to the National Archives in Washington, D.C., your costs should be limited.

This is a service which, for the most part, involves your time. You should have a typewriter (or have the material typed for you) and perhaps a postal box to handle the mail for this business.

Charge from $5 to $25 per page, depending on the difficulty of the subject. If, for instance, you are asked to produce 10,000 words on "Theories of Advertising in the 19th Century," you will require time to go to the library, pore through books on the history of advertising, then produce typewritten pages on this subject.

You should be adept at putting words together smoothly. Although your research will not necessarily depend on how skilled a creative writer you are, it will be necessary to present your information in the most readable form possible. If the report you are requested to produce is quite long you can consider reducing your rate per page slightly, but this will have to be at your discretion.

When you advertise, stress that you offer library research in *any* subject. If you have particular knowledge in an area such as history, literature, economics or another area of the humanities, you can mention your specialty in your advertisement. It will obviously be easier for you to produce research in a subject with which you have a working knowledge.

In addition to serving the academic community, pursue corporate clients by suggesting possible subjects that might be useful to them. For instance, you might discuss with the personnel officer of a corporation how valuable it would be to have a report on the new laws regarding workmen's compensation, social security payments, government-sponsored retirement benefits, or even investment opportunities.

If you are kept busy with your service and earn at a rate, say, of $10 a page, you can net as much as several hundred dollars a week. It is unlikely that you will be able to produce more than twenty typewritten pages a day, simply because of the physical limitations involved. And don't forget to allow time for the actual library hours involved in taking notes and searching out raw data.

Your largest audience will probably be from the college community, though you may find yourself serving clients from all over the country, if not the world. By advertising in national publications your service will be available on a nationwide basis. You may even get clients from abroad.

This service will require very little overhead. A supply of good bond paper and your typewriter are the basic tools. You will not, of course, need an office. You may not even have to have a telephone if you deal exclusively by mail.

If your service is successful you can hire others to perform different aspects of the research. The two students from Massachusetts who did so well servicing college students and teachers actually hired other students and teachers to do the research for them. They would find a professor or gifted student who had expertise in an area and pay a fee for written work which they would then mark up to net as much as 50 percent profit.

You probably won't be starting with a staff, so you may be best off by offering your service in subject areas in which you already have some background. By staying closer to areas you know, you'll be able to produce research more quickly and be better compensated for your time.

71 · Fence Installation

Millions of homes use fencing of all types, whether to protect a newly installed pool, to mark the boundary line of property, to enclose a patio, to create privacy or just to add visual appeal. Individuals and corporations use fences as varied as a two-foot-high garden fence to a twelve-foot-high wire fence for security purposes.

To get into this business of installing and repairing fencing you need a minimum of equipment and a good supply of able-bodied help. You can start your business with nothing more than a crowbar, shovel and post-hole digger. For jobs that require breaking through hard surfaces you may have to rent a jackhammer, but this will be the exception rather than the rule.

Fence installing is done most efficiently by at least two people. But even working with a part-time helper you can net yourself as much as $5 to $10 an hour. The drawback is that in many areas of the country this will be a seasonal business because cold weather makes cutting into the ground nearly impossible.

By arranging with a fence supplier to purchase materials, you can offer clients a complete package, fence *and* installation, for one flat rate. Make arrangements with a fence supplier to get your materials at as close to a wholesale rate as possible.

When estimating a fence job, your most important task will be to calculate the amount of time necessary for the installation. This requires close examination of the property to be fenced and may even mean you have to test the surface for hardness. If you have never done this kind of work, train by working for another fence installer.

In addition to direct selling to customers (through classified ads and a Yellow Pages listing), offer your service to fence suppliers who themselves sell to the public. You could even contract to do the work for fence suppliers who wish to provide their own customers with a complete service, from basic materials to finished installation.

You can start your installation business by servicing clients only on Saturdays and Sundays, especially if you want to work your way into this business gradually before giving up another job you might be holding now.

Probably the greatest risk in figuring an estimate for fence installation is calculating the time necessary to dig through the surface you will be sinking the fence into. If you live in New England, for instance, you can be pretty sure that you are going to hit rock at a shallow level. Take risks like this into account, test the ground thoroughly and base your estimate appropriately. The work is hard and you should be compensated on a basis of no less than $5 an hour. You should be able to hire unskilled part-time help for half that amount. If you have done a complete examination of the property to be fenced in, add another 15 percent to the time allotted to install, as your cushion against unforeseen obstacles.

The easiest type of permanent fence to install is a corral fence. This usually consists of fence post every eight feet connected by two or three horizontal pieces that fit into notches on the fence post. Probably the most difficult kind of fence to install is wire fence requiring steel poles which must be embedded in cement to maintain their rigidity. In addition to fencing in gardens and property demarcations, a growing number of homeowners are installing pools and tennis courts. Many states have laws requiring that pools be fenced in with a four-foot-high enclosure around the pool to protect it from incursion by children. Tennis court fencing is usually ten feet high, or higher, and may require special access routes to bring materials to the tennis court site.

You do not need a special vehicle of any type for this work. If you are offering a client a package deal, including materials, then arrange with the fence supplier to deliver materials to the job. Your own equipment should fit comfortably in a station wagon, if not your own automobile.

Assuming that the cold season means less business you still should be able to net $15,000 or more if you are able to keep busy when the ground is not frozen. This will be a full-time business at that income level. But even a part-time weekend business can net you up to $50 a day or more for most types of fence installation.

Once you are an experienced installer you may even be in a position to submit bids on major fence contracts, which could net you even greater profit. You have the advantage of not having to invest in materials until they are actually needed.

72 · Candy Kitchen

As with most food produced on a massive scale, the candy available from most store counters is just not nearly as good, tasty or rich as the homemade variety. An individual candy kitchen can be started in no more space than you already have in your kitchen at home. Whether your specialty is fudge or candy apples or butterscotch twists, the market is vast. America's sweet tooth has only grown in recent years and you can profit from this national craving.

The trick to your business is calculating the exact price of ingredients you put into your candy. You must become adept at figuring costs for small quantities of sugar, flavoring and other ingredients. When you have prepared a batch of your specialty, take it around to shops in your community. Of course, gourmet shops are the ideal market, as well as small grocery stores and variety stores. If you are selling candy by the box you can buy plain commercial boxes and have labels printed with your name on them stressing that this is *homemade* candy. The homemade nature of your candy is what will get the attention of buyers who want especially good-tasting sweets.

Take your samples to the outlets mentioned above, and if it is not boxed, bring a small hand-lettered sign that the merchant can place next to the candy saying something to the effect of, "Delicious Homemade Candy—All Natural Ingredients." Stress to your clients that you have added no preservatives or other chemicals.

A new area for the candy market has come in the form of artificially sweetened candy. Of course, you will not be able to advertise that the ingredients are all natural. Dietetic candy is usually far more expensive than regular sweets but actually will not cost you that much more. The market for imitation sugar has grown so quickly that manufacturers are now producing enough artificial sweeteners to compete favorably with the sugar producers. A batch of dietetic homemade candy will be unique and could provide you with a specialty business that gives your product an advantage over all others. Inquire about local licensing regulations for the selling of prepared food. This may not have anything to do with your business but it is safer to check than to risk losses later.

Price your candy by the piece or by the pound. Ask merchants to display the candy on a counter where it will get the most customer exposure. If you sell direct through advertising in your local newspaper, be careful not to underprice your commercial customers.

The market for your candy can expand as widely as the number of stores in which you are able to place it for sale. With a growing number of accounts you may want to add ovens or even rent commercial space to produce your product. As your business grows, keep in mind that your success has been based on the delicious homemade flavor of your product. The risk in quick growth is the temptation to mass produce. Although mass production may cost you less to produce your product, in the long run it will cost you more. Customers who buy your candy will only buy an inferior piece once.

As an additional outlet for sales you can develop a corporate clientele by offering a "Candy Gift" service. At Christmastime candy is a popular item for those who have to give large numbers of gifts and want to keep costs at a minimum. Homemade candy is a perfect gift item. You might even arrange to make custom-boxed candy with labels that are printed with the name of the giver.

73 · Collection Agency

Collection agencies are called in only when a creditor has just about given up all hope of collecting the debt himself. It can be an extremely profitable business, even on a small scale, because for every dollar you collect from a debtor you keep from 25¢ to 50¢ as your fee. Not all debts are collectable, of course, but when you are given an account for collection you are also given the opportunity of determining for yourself how much the debtor should pay to cancel the debt. In other words, if someone owes $1000 and you have discerned that this person will never be able to pay more than $500, you can agree to settle for that amount and still collect anywhere from $125 to $250 as your fee. Your client, the creditor, will consider himself lucky to have collected any portion of the debt.

Collection agencies succeed because they have become specialists in collecting money. Creditors do not have either the expertise or the time to go after debtors. As a beginner in the collection business you can service local professional people very effectively. Doctors, lawyers and others who are owed fees for their services are prime clients for your service.

To be successful in this business you must have tenacity and an aptitude for going after people relentlessly. The techniques employed by many collection agencies are under scrutiny by some government agencies and you should check with your local or state consumer bureau for guidelines on what is, or is not, permissible in the collection of a debt. For instance, you are not allowed to harass people unreasonably by calling them at all hours of the night. Therefore, most of your telephone collection business will have to take place during morning through early evening hours.

In addition to professionals like doctors and attorneys, solicit local department stores which offer charge accounts to their customers and even local banks that have Master Charge and BankAmericard services available. Banks are responsible individually for the debts of BankAmericard and Master Charge customers. It is not a national service.

You must be polite but firm in your collection efforts. Remember, these are debtors who have had months to pay a bill and have not done so. There are several books on collection techniques, and studying any one of these will give you a great deal of basic information. In addition to the telephone, you will be using the mail service to collect debts. There are specific ways to word letters to debtors that have proved to be most effective. These too can be studied in books that are probably available from your library.

Advertise for clients in the newspaper and Yellow Pages. Stress that you are a local service. Remember, you will not make any money except on those debts you collect. This is an appealing feature to your clients, since they have already given up on this debt.

Even a small collection agency can collect $5000 a month or more in old debts. If your fee is one-third of the amount collected, this will give you in excess of $1200 a month for your efforts. You do not need an office to run this service. You can work right out of your own home.

The telephone will be your most effective collection tool and you will probably need form letters which should be individually typed to each debtor. When you have exhausted your techniques for collection you have a last resort—small claims court, if the debt is $1000 or less. Check in your area for the small claims limit. Many communities have a limit of $500 or less. Once a judgment has been rendered against a debtor in small claims court, the full power of the legal system is put to use in your behalf. This involves garnishment of wages and other devices to extract money owed by a debtor.

Organize your business by first setting up a series of collection letters and developing techniques for phone collection. There are tested methods for dealing with debtors, well within the limits of the law. The best way to get training in this specialty is to work for a large collection agency. That agency has already developed proven techniques, and you can learn them while earning money at the same time.

74 · Community Center

If you have organizational talent and you enjoy bringing people together for mutually rewarding experiences, you could own and operate a profit-making center. You can run, and make money from, a community center even if you don't have facilities in your own home. Of course, if you happen to have a finished basement in your house, large enough to accommodate a group of children or adults (say a maximum of twenty people), you have the basic tools right at hand.

The purpose of your community center is to provide a setting and activities to involve young and older people in an array of games, meetings, educational opportunities, even counseling. If your own home is not suitable for group get-togethers, you can usually rent, at a nominal fee, meeting rooms in a church or "Y" or even an unused area in the back of a store. The important thing is not where you meet (as long as the surroundings are clean and light), but the kinds of activities you promote.

Begin by giving your center a name, then advertise in your local newspaper. Your center should appeal to all age groups, so you may run several different ads appealing to separate age levels. Here's one ad, for instance: "Senior Citizen Social Group Now Being Formed. Fairhaven Community Center. Call 784-1873 For More Information." Or: "Attention High School Students! Club House Now Being Started At Fairhaven Community Center. Games, Recreation, Outings, Personal-Problem Counseling. Call 784-1873 For Information."

For each age group to whom you want to appeal, you will plan activities, bring in guest speakers, offer instruction, and just generally provide a place where people with similar interests can get together socially. Although most communities already have a YMCA or YWCA, as well as other kinds of public social centers, these centers tend to cater to a very broad cross-section of the population, and are usually charitable in their origins. A private club, which is legally what your community center would be, has more flexibility. It is not under the same restrictions as a public facility.

Check the local regulations regarding licensing for a private center.

Charge monthly or even annual dues for membership in your center. A rate of $2.50 a week, $10 a month or $100 a year per member will give you enough start-up capital to begin business. In addition to these dues, you can charge additional sums for specific activities. If, for instance, you are planning a guest talk by a professional retirement counselor (for your senior citizen members), charge a nominal $2 for each member who wants to attend this event. An admission charge serves two purposes: Those who don't want to attend don't feel that their dues are paying for other people's benefits, and you can profit on individual activities that may appeal only to a small segment of the membership.

Your profit potential in this socially minded business is quite substantial. If you start with fifty members paying dues of, say, $100 a year, you have a basic fund of $5000. Then, if you organize just two activities a week that net you $40 each, you net another $4000 annually. Special activities, like annual bridge or backgammon tournaments, in which entrance fees are paid and prizes awarded, could bring in as much as $500 profit in themselves.

As a private club, you could also sell liquor to adult members (carefully check local license regulations), as well as hold dances and other profit-making celebrations.

With even a small nucleus of members and thoughtfully planned activities, you could clear $15,000 or more in a year. For groups like senior citizens, teen-agers and others with special interests, you will be providing a pleasant meeting place at a reasonable rate. Community service can, in this case, be both helpful and profitable.

75 · Locksmith

This is a particularly good business for someone who is retired or semiretired, does not want to work full time, yet would like to develop a skill that can pay well and requires little overhead.

Your requirements are a good set of specialized tools and, of course, the skill to use these tools effectively. If you enjoy tinkering, if you've ever repaired clocks, guns, even toasters (as an amateur), then you probably have the aptitude for locksmithing. You can get specialized training in this skill from books, from mail-order courses, or (and this is the best way) by working with a skilled locksmith.

A regular, small classified ad and a listing in the Yellow Pages will constitute sufficient advertising. You do not have to have a retail outlet for your service. A home workshop will do. Make it clear in your ads that you make housecalls. And, as you'll see if you look in the Yellow Pages under "Locksmith," if you name your service AAAA-Locksmith, you'll get a front listing. This is valuable for acquiring emergency-service customers who usually call the first name they come to when a house- or car-key is lost.

Locksmithing is skilled work, but does not require years of apprenticeship, as, for instance, plumbing would. If your service is available on a 24-hour emergency basis, as it should be, you will be able to command as much as $20 for a single housecall.

Tools can cost more than $100, and if you acquire key duplicating equipment, grinding wheels and other shop machinery, those costs can double or triple. But you need only make this investment once, and tools and shop equipment can frequently be paid out over a period of time.

In addition to servicing, you can sell locks, safes and other specialized hardware right from your shop, without investing in a retail location. As your list of customers and your experience grow, you can offer a security consultation service, expanding your capabilities to involve burglar and fire alarm installation, safe and vault work and other services in the field of home and business security.

This is a business which will grow slowly but steadily. It can be started as a part-time service, which means you can get your training while earning an income from your regular job. Locksmithing itself does not usually demand heavy lifting or intense strenuous effort. Rather, it is intricate work which requires delicacy and an ability to manipulate small metal parts.

As a part-time locksmith you could earn as much as $5000 or more a year working just a few hours a week. With an expanded service, in the field of private and commercial security and retail sales of security equipment, your income can grow to $20,000 a year or more, with little investment except your time to acquire professional skill.

76 · *Business Skills School*

"Business skills" is really an umbrella title which means typing and shorthand. In every community in this country there seems to be a constant need for skilled secretarial help, even during times of economic stress. Almost every business and professional person needs an individual, in or out of the office, to take dictation and type quickly and skillfully. But secretaries are not the only ones who can use these skills effectively. Journalists, students, even police officers who have to type daily reports are just a few examples of people who find typing skills a very helpful talent to possess.

You can start your own business skills school right in your home, without risking much cash. Your investment at the beginning requires that you purchase ten to twenty desks or tables, typing paper, steno notebooks and a supply of pencils. You can rent typewriters on a monthly basis, usually for $10 to $20 each per month, depending on prevailing rates in your community. Or, you can try to arrange for reduced-rental "loaners" from a local office machine supplier, in exchange perhaps for a promise to refer students to this supplier exclusively.

The first thing to do is outline your own courses for typing and shorthand (make them two separate courses). To do this effectively, it will pay you to have taken a typing course yourself, whether or not you already possess typing skills. There is no better way to learn how a business skills school operates.

Once you have outlined a course of instruction, acquired the necessary desks or tables and lined up a source for rental typewriters, you're ready to advertise for students. In your local newspaper ad, stress that your school is for *anyone* who wants to learn this important skill. And list the different ways typing can be useful to secretaries, college students, professional writers, owners of small businesses, even doctors, lawyers and police personnel.

An additional service you can offer your students (and this should be emphasized in your ads) is a secretarial placement service upon completion of the course. With the demand for secretarial help always seeming to outrun the supply, you can add to the appeal of your school, as well as profit from this specialized em-

ployment service. All it takes is regular contact with personnel departments of large companies in your area, or even an arrangement with another local employment agency to supply them with skilled graduates of your school. The call for good secretaries being what it is, this is one employment arrangement in which the employer almost always willingly pays the agency fee.

The tuition rates for your school should, of course, be competitive with other schools in the area. If you've taken a course at one of these schools you should have a good idea of the going rates. A ten-week course, with classes held one evening a week for two hours, can command fees of $150 or more. With ten students in each class, you can run three, four or five courses simultaneously and gross as much as $7500 in one ten-week period.

With the rental of ten machines at a cost of, say, $150 a month, plus the cost of paper and pencils running another $25 a month, your expenses will be less than $500 for the ten-week period. Using a room in your home as a classroom can net you over $700 a week!

If your instruction is good (and that will be determined by the success of the typists you turn out), and your service is above average, you do not have to offer the lowest rates in town to become very successful. People who want to learn typing and/or shorthand would rather be assured that their instruction is tops, not just available at bargain-basement rates. Offer a placement service in addition to instruction and you have implied to your students that you'll not only train them, but you'll be helping them turn their skill into money right away.

The key to your success with this business will be based on how much use you get from the machines you rent or buy. Aside from a slightly greater cost for maintenance, you are really paying the same for the machine whether it's used for two hours a week or twenty hours. Keep your typewriters busy and your income can reach the $50,000 bracket in a surprisingly short period of time.

77 · Professional Sound Recording

There has been a revolution of sorts in the sound recording business. With the technology for inexpensive recording devices having improved remarkably in recent years, the desire and need for tape-recorded records of various events has also grown. Many people want to have a permanent record of important social occasions, like wedding ceremonies, bar mitzvah services, communion services, confirmations, even children's birthday parties. Businesses are looking to tape recordings as a way to preserve important speeches by executives, minutes of board meetings and other events. Even some courts of law are now committing trial proceedings to recording tape instead of stenographic tape.

With good tape recorders, both cassette and reel-to-reel, available for less than $100, you could fill this new and growing need for a very small investment. Pay a visit to a professional sound equipment supplier, if there is one in your area, or to a good retail outlet that has a wide selection of quality tape recorders. You will need a recorder that is easily portable but not too small to provide excellent sound quality. Just as important as the recording device itself is the kind of microphone you use. Sensitive mikes can sometimes cost as much as the tape recorder.

Explain to the (hopefully expert) supplier that you need equipment that can provide quality recording in a number of different situations. In addition to recording just spoken words, you will have to allow for situations in which voices may be coming from several directions (thus the need for a sensitive microphone) and at different volumes. You may also need to record music and singing, which should come through the tape clearly, even at high volume.

Start with one good tape recorder and as many as two, three or four different microphones which can be used for various recording situations. As you become more involved in this business you'll probably find that you will want more and more specialized mikes and other devices. But at the beginning anyway, keep your equipment investment at the minimum necessary to achieve reasonable quality.

Wherever you purchase your equipment, make sure you receive

thorough instruction in its use. Spend as much time as possible practicing in the store, while the supplier watches. Ask all the questions you can think of, and call on the telephone later if you have further questions. This supplier, who stands to make a profit from your purchase, is one of the few people who will give you free assistance. Take full advantage of it.

Now you're ready to advertise and publicize your service. The newspaper and Yellow Pages will be your basic media (with a listing under "Recording Service"). Your rates should be based on the degree of sophistication needed. For recording a business speech or meeting, charge at least $10 an hour. Your charges start when you arrive on location and end when you leave. In other words, you get paid for set-up time as well as actual recording time. If you are recording a concert, where you might need more than one microphone, as well as mixing skills and other sound engineering techniques, your rates can be as high as $25 an hour or more.

Until you gain substantial practice in this business, limit yourself to the simple recording jobs which involve less elaborate equipment and training. As you become more skilled and can invest in more expensive equipment, your service capabilities will increase (and so will your income). You may soon find that you have the means to set up your own recording studio, either at home or in a rented space. But you are advised to start modestly. Studio recording equipment costs many thousands of dollars.

Even with an inauspicious start, you can earn several hundred dollars a week—working completely from your own home, with travel to various locations.

78 · Decorative Accessories

Wall plaques, decorative screens, simple cabinets, storage boxes, trundle beds, "manufactured" memorabilia, framed posters—these are all relatively easy items to manufacture with a minimum of handwork aptitude. These kinds of accessories are not outrageously expensive and can be created to suit the needs of an individual home.

If you have even an amateur carpenter's skill, plus a dose of decorating imagination, you can build a business to serve individual homeowners, interior decorators and even the retail accessory market. You need a basement or garage workshop and a set of tools. Your tools—hammer, screwdrivers, small saws (including a jigsaw or saber saw), pliers, etc.—are the type owned by most people who perform their own simple home repairs.

Advertise your custom accessory-building service in the classified section of the newspaper. When you receive a call from a client, make an appointment to visit this prospective buyer at his or her home. Go prepared not only to give estimates for specific work, but to offer your own contribution to the decorating problems this client may have. You'll be part decorating consultant and part craftsman in this situation.

If a blank wall needs imaginative treatment, suggest accessories (that you can build) to complement the decor of the rest of the room.

Take photographs of the jobs you have completed and use them to suggest ideas to other clients. You don't need elaborate photo equipment. An Instamatic will do, and color pictures will form an excellent portfolio of your work.

Molded plaster wall plaques, small screens and other "portable" accessories can also be sold through retail outlets. Take samples of this work to gift shops, retail lumber stores, kitchen cabinet suppliers and others who sell home improvement goods. Take photos of these items and your larger custom screens, built-ins and storage boxes to interior decorators. The retail outlets you visit may agree to sell your goods on consignment, or even stock them as inventory. Interior decorators may recommend your services to their clients, or even call you in as part of a decorating job.

For your custom in-home work, charge a fee based on your estimate of time plus cost of materials. If calculating the time necessary to complete a job is very difficult, you can charge on a materials-plus-time basis. The client pays for materials as they are purchased and you receive an hourly rate for your time. You should get from $5 to $10 an hour for this work. For plaques and other items you create in your shop, set your price according to size and detail. Shop the stores in your area to get a feel for competitive prices, and act accordingly.

You can pick up dozens of creative suggestions by browsing through *House and Garden* and other home decorating magazines. You can also use these publications to suggest ideas to clients. You should be able to construct most of the accessories illustrated by using ingenuity.

This is a specialized business in which you can offer the advantages of designer and builder at the same time. Between custom work and retail sales you can net over $200 a week. When the demand for custom work slows down, pick up the slack by making accessories for retail sale. Balancing your output will protect you during the slower seasons.

79 · Cosmetic/Fashion Coordinator

This is a unique, fascinating consultation service which will be most successful if you live in or near a large city. A cosmetic/fashion coordinator is an advisor in personal appearance. If you have a special sense of what enhances people's appearance, if you can define what it is in a garment that will make a woman look taller, or slimmer, you have the aptitude to consult professionally.

This kind of business will draw clients only from a large cosmopolitan area. If you have had no training in either makeup or fashion coordination, you can learn in one of two ways. You can read books on color coordination, clothing design, application of cosmetics and makeup, or you can train "on the job," in a beauty salon, a clothing store, a fashion design center, a wig shop, or any of an array of retail and manufacturing outlets that are involved in a person's appearance in some way.

Chances are, if you've ever worked as a clerk in an apparel shop, or even done amateur theatrical makeup, you already have a basic sense of how to alter or enhance a person's appearance. Cosmetologists (makeup advisors) and fashion coordinators can have individual, private clients, as well as commercial free-lance accounts like manufacturers and exclusive retail outlets. As a private consultant to clients, your job is to advise a person on a wardrobe, makeup (or no makeup) and hints to enhance personal appearance. In a sense, you are to the individual what an interior decorator is to a room.

To start your business, take a classified ad that might read something like this: "Professional cosmetologist/fashion coordinator will put together a new you. Consultations on makeup, wardrobes to bring out your beauty. Call 519-8762 for appointment at your home."

Like an interior decorator, you will visit clients personally, discuss the client's appearance and suggest makeup and wardrobe hints based on the individual's needs. Some clients will even want you to do their wardrobe shopping for them, just as a decorator would shop for furniture and accessories.

It will be either a fee-based business (an hourly consultation rate) in which you charge from $15 to $25 per hour, or your fee can be based on a percentage (15 percent) of the total cost of a new wardrobe. Regardless of the time involved, you should receive a minimum of $30 to $50 per consultation.

In addition to serving private clients, your services will be needed by clothing shops, organizations throwing a fashion show, cosmetic salons, beauty salons, and manufacturers who need professional advice on fashion coordination. Good coordinators can command fees in the hundreds of dollars for just one job. As a consultation business, you need no office, just a telephone and business cards.

Like most consultants, your business will grow in proportion to the personal referrals you receive. Your service is an advisory business in which personal reputation is the cement that holds it together. With success, you enjoy greater demand, and your fees can provide you with an income in excess of $20,000 a year. Clients who have benefited from your advice will consider your help priceless.

80 · Advertising Specialties

Advertising specialties, also called premiums, are inexpensive novelties or gifts given away by many, many businesses, both retail and manufacturing, to publicize their name and leave a reminder with customers. The novelties are usually imprinted with the giver's name and are usually something useful, like a calendar or ballpoint pen—an item that will be used frequently and act as a reminder to the recipient.

The specialty business is a multimillion-dollar business whose greatest returns are at Christmastime, when the ad specialties serve as a holiday gift that is inexpensive and can be distributed to large numbers of customers or even employees.

The items most frequently imprinted are plastic memo books, calendars, pens, coin holders, plastic rain bonnets, inexpensive lighters, key chains, pen knives and plastic coffee mugs. As a distributor and seller of these imprinted novelty items, you sell to retailers, gas stations and others who sell to the public. You can also sell these items to large and small manufacturers who either use the items to send to their customers or as small tokens to employees at holiday gift-giving time. Sometimes these novelties are sold by retailers, with or without a name imprint, as low-priced convenience items.

As a seller, you do not put up any money until you have a firm order from your customer. You then send your order to an advertising specialty manufacturer, who returns the product to you, imprinted. You deliver the order to your customer who pays you at the time of delivery.

Although the great bulk of novelty items cost less than 25¢, there are occasions when a large manufacturer, for instance, may want a more impressive novelty gift for his customers. A set of six highball glasses may cost the manufacturer as much as $3 or more (with the manufacturer's name or logo in color on each glass), which then provide a truly impressive gift to customers who may be giving the manufacturer thousands of dollars in business each year.

Your first job is to locate several novelty manufacturers who will serve your needs. Consult the Yellow Pages from a large city telephone directory, the classified section of major newspapers, or visit the library and ask for a directory of manufacturers. Choose the manufacturers who can provide you with a good variety of novelty items, costing you from 5¢ to $1 each. Write to the manufacturer and ask for samples with your own name (or your company name) imprinted. Explain that you will be selling these items as personalized novelties, that you expect to be reordering frequently. In many cases, the manufacturer will send you free samples for distribution, but you should be prepared to pay for your samples in any case. Once you have a good selection of different items (which should cost you less than $100, even if you're paying for samples), start making personal visits to every retail and manufacturing outlet in your area. Leave a sample if you don't get an order right away. This will be your calling card, and will have your name imprinted, along with your phone number. Also leave a mimeographed sheet listing the complete line of advertising specialities you offer. When you get an order be sure you have promised a delivery date that can be met. Nothing will dampen a customer's enthusiasm faster than a missed delivery.

In addition to personal calls, take classified or display ads in as many publications as you can afford, including inexpensive classifieds in national magazines and metropolitan newspapers. But when dealing by mail with customers you have never seen, be sure to get a deposit from those clients. You must cover yourself particularly well at the start of your business venture because you will not be able to afford collection fees should your mail customers default.

The advertising specialty business is low unit price, but big volume sales. You may get an order for ballpoint pens, imprinted, that cost only 12¢ each. But that order could easily be for 5000 pens. If the pens cost you 6¢ each you have netted $300 from that one sale. Not bad for a day's work.

More than anything else, this business requires perseverance and more perseverance. You've got to go out there every day and try to make sales. The one time you slack off and skip a store may be the sale of a lifetime. And someone else may make that sale while you're catching a movie!

The volume of the novelty business being what it is, your venture can grow very quickly once you start clicking. Individuals who have started out going from store to store have grown to enormous size within a short time, netting $50,000 a year or more—on sales of 12¢ pens!

81 · Landscape Services

Most residents of suburban areas, whether they mow their own lawns or not, need help at some time or other with landscape maintenance and/or complete garden care. Because this business requires little investment and can be learned quickly, it is one of the most competitive businesses around. But if you're ready to use imaginative techniques to get customers, and you enjoy working outdoors, you can make a tidy income in a high-profit market.

Your cash investment for garden tools is small. You need a power lawn mower (a rotary type will do), rakes, hedge clippers, pruning shears and hoes. If you don't already own a set of these tools, try to buy secondhand equipment from power mower shops which take trade-ins, garage sales and classified ads from homeowners selling out.

It would be helpful to have a small pickup truck, both to transport tools and helpers to a job, and to remove brush and leaves from the job to the dump (or landfill area). But if you don't have a truck, a station wagon will do for starters. If you need a larger vehicle for occasional use, rent a U-Haul trailer or some other small trailer on a one-day basis as needed. Your only need for this larger carrying space will be to remove waste from a land site on which you are working.

Here are the kinds of services you will offer to your customers: lawn maintenance and weeding, leaf removal, hedge and shrub clipping, raking, cleaning underbrush, low-branch removal (not tree surgery), garden maintenance (flower and vegetable gardens), tilling (to prepare land for gardening, in which case you rent a rototiller a day at a time), edging, sweeping, fertilizing. And in winter, although it will be less busy, peat moss insulation for shrubs and flowerbeds, snow removal and sidewalk shoveling, salting steps, porches, sidewalks, snow plowing (if you either own or can rent a jeep and plow).

Charge your customers on a flat-fee basis, whether your service is called for a one-time visit or a contract service in which you maintain land on a regular basis. Estimating your work can be tricky. You must have part-time help, which should be easy to get in the form of students off from school in the summer. Working under your supervision, you hire unskilled labor at about $2.50 an hour.

You may underestimate jobs at the beginning of your business, but experience will be a fast teacher. Work only once at a loss, and you'll be unlikely to make the same mistake again. Since this business is so competitive, your rates will play a big part in the ease with which you get jobs. When estimating a job to your customer, make sure you explain fully every service you will perform. Itemize weeding, raking, cutting, clean-up, sweeping—all as part of your service. It will make the job seem large and important, and will give you an edge over the landscape service that says, "Oh, we'll do the whole lawn for $125." When giving an estimate, arrive at a figure that is not even. Instead of saying $125, say $126.75. It will look like you've been very careful and have figured the job down to the penny.

When actually calculating your costs, don't forget to figure in the fuel and time needed to get back and forth to the site.

Be an aggressive advertiser. Place attention-getting classified ads. Guarantee satisfaction for your service. Stress that your rates are the lowest in the area for quality work. Place business cards in mailboxes. List all the *specific* services you perform. Don't just say "Lawn Maintenance," say "Weeding, Cutting, Raking, Sweeping," etc. That will give the impression that you do *more* than just "maintain," whatever that means.

Calculate your costs to perform a job, then add from 30 percent to 60 percent as profit, whether or not you are actually doing the lawn work yourself. If you work long days during the spring, summer and fall, you can make enough to work part-time, or not at all, during the winter months when outdoor work comes to a standstill. Look for ways to cut even small costs. If you can dump leaves and weeds in a hole where someone has asked for landfill, you save fees at the town dump.

Busy landscape services can net their owners $20,000 or more just for three-season work. The point is to work harder and offer more than your competition.

82 · Guidebook Publishing

Almost every area in this country has restaurants, entertainment, sightseeing and picnic grounds, recreation, museums, historical sites, amusement parks, golf courses and dozens of other diversions for public enjoyment. There are also, of course, police stations, hospitals, bus terminals, airports and many other public services.

For area residents, as well as vacationers and business travelers passing through your area, there may be no way of finding all the services available without checking a multitude of sources. A guidebook is a valuable help for locating any service an individual needs in one handy place. You can put together such a book with no investment (except your time) by preselling the guidebook before you have to spend money to print it.

The first thing to do, of course, is to prepare a listing of all the services available in your area, from restaurants to dry cleaners to all-night drugstores. You divide your listings into categories, and for each category you write a small paragraph describing the special nature of the service, the address, phone number, hours of business and any other comments that are pertinent. Under "Restaurants" you list the name, the types of food served, the average price for meals, the atmosphere, the kind of clients the restaurant serves (for instance, "good for family dining" or "businessman's haven"), and you can even rate the establishment.

Putting this listing together is time-consuming, but once it's done you have created a product that will be current for six months to a year from the time of publication. With use of the Yellow Pages, you can locate most businesses and services in your area. Your job will be to make a firsthand investigation of these services, then report on them in your guidebook.

Once you have your information, presell the book to local merchants (who may want to give it away free) at the same time that you solicit advertisements to appear in the book. Hotels, motels, service stations and other travel stops are good potential marketplaces for the book.

Once you have received orders, in writing, for copies of the book, take your manuscript to a printer who will help you lay it out, as well as set type and print for you. Be sure to print a retail price on the cover that is at least twice the price you are asking from your commercial customer for each copy. If you sell bulk copies to a hotel or restaurant for 25¢ or 50¢, put a price of $1 on the cover.

If you print 1000 copies of your guidebook, and it is 32 pages, 5½ x 8½ in size, your costs will be about 15¢ each. If you sell the book to commercial clients for 35¢ or 50¢ you will net between $200 and $350 for 1000 copies. After your wholesale market is filled, offer the book in classified ads for full list price, $1. You can always reprint when your supply is exhausted. If you accept advertising, your profit can jump substantially. And every year you can update the book in far less time than it took to put it together from scratch.

One thousand copies should be your minimum print run. When you print greater quantities, your cost per book will be less. Although you may not become an overnight millionaire from this business, you can net from several hundred to several thousand dollars for a few weeks' work.

83 · Flea Market/Art Show Organizer

An interesting business has grown up in recent years because of the public's increasing desire for art, crafts and secondhand merchandise at reasonable prices. The best way to acquire these goods is for someone to visit an artist's studio or antique shop or thrift shop. But most communities have few if any of these shops. And even if there are a few outlets available, they usually offer only the work of a few artists, craftsmen and purveyors of secondhand goods.

An answer to this problem has come about with once-a-week markets in shopping center parking lots or enclosed mall lobbies, where the work of literally hundreds of artists and dealers is available in one place. The way it works is this: An organizer (either an individual or sometimes a charity) announces to artists and craftsmen all over the area that they can "rent" an outdoor (or indoor) space on a given day, frequently a Sunday, at such-and-such a shopping center. The artists and other sellers who want to participate pay an "entrance fee" of $10 each. And for all work that they sell, they pay the organizer an additional 10 percent commission.

This gives the public an opportunity to see and purchase work directly from hundreds of artists, craftsmen and antique dealers at one time, in one place. The artists usually have separate showings on one Sunday, and the next Sunday may be given over to the sellers of flea market merchandise.

The sellers get a chance to sell directly to the public without renting permanent retail space, and the public enjoys buying direct from artists and others in a joyful, carnival-like setting.

To organize your own art show and/or flea market requires that you first enlist enough sellers to fill a large open area. You then contract with a shopping center to use a portion of their parking area, usually on a Sunday when retail stores will be closed. Then you advertise this open-air market to the public.

If you get fifty artists and craftsmen to display at one of these markets, you get $500 as entrance fees. The artists bring their own vehicles, usually a station wagon, van or car. They set up tables in a small area assigned to each and offer their wares. Your cost for renting the parking area is usually nominal, say $100, because it is space that would go unused on a Sunday anyway. So, even before the show opens, you have netted $400 before advertising. If you allot another $100 for classified ads, posters and other announcements, you're starting in the black. Then, you collect a 10 percent commission on all goods sold. All payments should be made to a central cashier who will issue receipts with which purchaser will redeem his merchandise. It is not unusual for an artist to sell from $100 to $1000 worth of work on a given day. Multiply your 10 percent commission by 5 (the number of artist-participants) and you could easily net $2000 or more for your efforts as organizer!

Flea markets would work the same way, of course, only your audience of potential participants is much wider. Virtually anyone who has useful, small household goods or antiques to sell is a possible participant in this one-day selling venture.

One organizer, World Art Tours, has actually set up a complete display circuit along the East Coast. Artists will travel sometimes hundreds of miles to show their work, under the supervision of World Art Tours, in shopping plazas from Maine to Florida. With a stable of artists and craftsmen willing to travel, you can eliminate the effort to round up local talent in each community. And the artists are delighted because they have an extremely low overhead for their joint retail outlet.

With organizational ability, and with very little risk, you can profit to the tune of $50,000 a year or more in a business that is still known to only a few people.

84 · Manufacturer's Representative

Manufacturers are developing new products constantly, at a rate of thousands each year. For smaller manufacturers in particular, one of the problems in new product development is national representation. If you are a talented salesperson and can motivate others to sell, you can develop your own business as an exclusive distributor of products in your area.

The first step is to locate new products you feel can be sold well. There are two ways to go about this: The first is to read business magazines and newspapers like the *Wall Street Journal*, the *New York Times* (Sunday business section especially), the *Los Angeles Times* and other major metropolitan papers. Manufacturers looking for national distribution advertise in these publications. The second way to develop leads on new products is to travel. Various industries hold sales conventions in different parts of the country each year where new products are displayed. But you can also be a wise shopper. If you are on vacation, browse through local shops and see what kinds of unusual or new merchandise are available. If something strikes you as having good potential, and you haven't seen that product for sale in your area, look on the label to see who manufactures the item.

Contact the manufacturers of products you discover through the news media, or through personal observation. State that you would like to have exclusive rights to sell and distribute that product in your area. Usually, the only requirement for an exclusive contract to distribute in an untapped area is that your sales not fall below a certain dollar volume. Assuming your credentials as a salesperson are good, you offer a no-risk investment on the part of the manufacturer. You are paid only on a commission basis, for products sold and delivered.

By getting exclusive distribution rights to several products, especially if they are related, you can become an efficient, profitable representative. It makes sense to acquire exclusive rights to more than one product. If you become the representative for a manufacturer of a desk lamp, for instance, you should try to supplement your line by representing a manufacturer of long-life light bulbs, or ceiling fixtures, or other items that you can sell to a light fixture retailer at the same time that you sell your desk lamps. You have to be careful not to take on competitive lines, as this will diminish your value to both manufacturers of the similar products.

Your commission ranges from 3 percent to 7 percent, depending on the price of the items you sell, and the expected volume from each sale. Once business warrants it, you can hire other salespeople to work for you. In addition to the commissions from your own sales efforts, you get an override from the sales of those who work for you. Manufacturers' representatives who enjoy even moderate success net from $15,000 to over $100,000 a year in commissions and overrides. A profitable business indeed!

85 · Professional Flower/Plant Service

Few businesses work on as high a percentage of profit as florists, not because flower sellers are more greedy than other retailers, but simply because their prices are based on the spoilage rate of cut flowers. Regardless of the reasons, there is a way you can capitalize on the extra mark-up without the disadvantage of high spoilage. By servicing businesses with regular fresh-flower and plant supply deliveries, you can enjoy a guarantee that no florist can count on for sure—you can sell everything you buy.

Start with a classified ad directed to all businesses in your area, retailers and offices alike, offering to supply fresh flowers on a regular basis. Make personal solicitations to large companies, doctors' offices, law offices, insurance company suites—virtually anyone whose interests are served by having attractive waiting rooms and lobbies. For an agreed-upon sum each week, you deliver bouquets of fresh flowers to the various locations you have under contract. You might stimulate business by offering a free vase upon the signing of a trial contract of, say, six months.

You can hire a messenger service to make your deliveries, although you'd be better advised to make deliveries yourself until business is good. You need only a station wagon to hold boxes of flowers, which you unpack and arrange right on your customer's premises.

To purchase flowers and flowering plants, you must locate the nearest wholesale flower market in your area. These markets operate daily or weekly, and open for business early in the morning, usually at 4 or 5 A.M.

This is a good business to start while you hold a regular day job. You can purchase your flowers early and even deliver them on Saturday or Sunday, if you can gain access to your clients' offices.

Your prices can remain competitive with local retail florists and still bring you a handsome profit. Remember, you will not suffer from spoilage losses since you purchase only the flowers you have presold. Check retail florists. You should be able to buy a dozen roses for as little as 50¢ at the wholesale market. And you can command rates as high as $3.50 a dozen and still avoid the danger of pricing yourself out of the market.

In addition to contract sales to offices and retail outlets like fine clothing and jewelry stores, you can service individual homeowners. Of course, you should limit your private homeowner solicitations to more affluent areas, as this is a luxury which is likely to sell well only to those in high-income brackets.

You can also offer all your clients a plant-decorating service. These will be one-time sales, but the mark-up on green plants is only slightly lower than on fresh-cut flowers. One plant decoration contract can net you several hundred dollars alone. Your fresh-cut flower delivery service can bring you $40 a day profit, after paying for flowers and fuel to deliver them, for part-time efforts. With full-time participation, combined with a plant-decoration service and even sales of decorative vases and plant pots, you could clear several hundred dollars a week.

Try to get paid for your deliveries on a weekly basis, preferably at the time you deliver. If your larger corporate clients balk at this kind of payment schedule, then you have to be willing to bill for your service. But do not let bills run more than forty days without payment. Like fresh flowers, bills can go bad quickly.

Once your business is under way, solicit your accounts for flower service on special occasions—Christmas parties, even weddings and other celebrations. These special services will tie in well to your contract business and can bring you hundreds of dollars in added profit for each occasion.

86 · Self-Improvement Seminars

The recent and enormous popularity of techniques such as Transactional Analysis and Transcendental Meditation has caused many large and small corporations (as well as millions of individuals) to consider these special methods to increase employee output. The reasoning is really quite simple: If workers are communicating better and feeling better they will be more productive.

If you have ever participated in TA or TM therapy, and you have felt the benefits of these techniques, you could become an effective seminar leader yourself. National organizations have been set up by advocates of both TA and TM, with facilities to train people to lead others. Training centers proliferate in most states, especially on the East and West Coasts.

Training to become a seminar leader can be completed in a week or two. Once successfully completed, you should have the credentials to organize and run seminars with up to fifteen persons attending each seminar.

Your market for training others will be both corporations and groups of private individuals who want to form their own groups. First, the potential among business clients:

Make appointments to visit personnel directors at all the large companies in your area. Come prepared to discuss the benefits of your seminars, as well as to show the teaching materials you will use. (Kits have been put together by national TA and TM groups specifically for this purpose.) Explain to the personnel directors that your training sessions can actually produce higher profits for the company by achieving several goals—greater employee output, better employee-employer communications, and better participation by workers in helping to solve company problems. You will be successful if you can convince these personnel directors that the benefits to the company are substantial and material.

Seminars run in behalf of businesses can net you several hundred dollars for each series (usually five to ten meetings). Materials to use with seminar participants are readily available from national TA and TM organizations.

Private groups have frequently gotten together for the purpose of pooling the funds of individuals to hire a seminar leader. Several friends or relatives chip in $20 or more each. They hire a seminar leader, usually for one marathon session.

In addition to personal solicitations, it will pay to advertise in trade journals read by leaders of various industries, and magazines like *Psychology Today*, which is read by lay persons and professionals alike.

If you can get an exclusive franchise to lead seminars in your community or region, you will have the benefit of using prepared materials proven successful by nationwide organizations of TA and TM enthusiasts. Use one client as a recommendation to sell other corporate clients. Your fees, with regular seminar work, can amount to hundreds of dollars a week in net profit.

87 · Homemade Jams and Jellies

If you have ever made jams and jellies for friends, relatives or simply for gifts to others, you are probably already aware of the appreciation people display for homemade preserves. If you have yet to prepare your own preserves, you can learn how by buying one of the many books on the subject, or by writing to the U.S. Department of Agriculture for a brochure that gives easy-to-follow instructions.

You can start and operate a small business in preserves right from your own kitchen. To run your business efficiently you should buy fresh fruits in quantity during their peak seasons. In most parts of the country this will mean your busiest work periods will be during summer and early fall. Plan your time so that you put up your preserves in one concentrated period of time, say a month or two, from late July to late September. Then spend the following months selling your goods.

Because of the rising popularity of homemade preserves, there have been periodic shortages of canning lids. You'd be wise to stock up on these kinds of supplies when the public demand is lowest.

Once you have prepared and preserved your quantities of peach jam, apple butter, grape jelly and other specialties, it's time to start selling. Take samples of your goods to local gourmet and gift shops, small grocers and other specialty stores. Let the proprietors of these various retail outlets try a sample of your favorite jam or jelly. It's a good sales technique, and a good way to enhance the relationship between you and your customer. Keep as much of an inventory as you can manage at your home, in anticipation of the peak selling season between Thanksgiving and New Year's Day.

Be sure to check with your local or state health department for licensing requirements for food sellers.

Besides selling to retailers, you can promote a brisk business with direct sales to consumers. Advertise in your local newspaper, place posters in conspicuous locations and spread the news by word-of-mouth advertising. As long as your prices do not undercut your retail outlets' prices, you can manage both kinds of sales easily.

If your output allows it, you might try handwritten labels, which will emphasize the homemade nature of your products. (The labeled jars themselves might become attractive decorator items after the preserves have been eaten.)

Your income from this business will be moderate, simply because a home kitchen can only produce a limited quantity of goods. But you can supplement this income while you are producing preserves by running canning classes at the same time. Classes of five or six students, paying $1.50 per student per class, can produce an additional income of $35 a week. If you are selling preserves for at least twice the cost of your materials (including containers) you could clear a combined profit of as much as $150 or more a week.

88 · Private Tutoring Service

If you have ever taught professionally, or even if you've helped your children do their homework, you can earn a good income as a private tutor. The market for this service is vaster than most people realize. Students having problems with one or another subject in public school, handicapped youngsters (either with learning or emotional disabilities), students who must stay out of school for extended periods of time (because of accidents or injuries), adults who had to stop their educations prematurely, people who want to study a language in anticipation of a trip abroad, or for business purposes—all are prime candidates for private tutoring.

The first thing to do is determine what areas of study you are qualified to tutor. If you have a college degree in one of the humanities, you are probably able to teach English grammar and literature, history, philosophy, and perhaps even sociology and economics. If you plan to concentrate on tutoring younger children, you can teach most subjects, including elementary arithmetic, spelling and reading. If you have a mathematical background in college, or even if you have been a bookkeeper as part of your adult career, you can teach principles of accounting and economics, as well as algebra, geometry and math. The point is to examine all your education and work experience and find those areas you have in common with today's educational needs.

Of course, you can relate your own working experience in a very practical way by tutoring adults in career skills like advertising, small-business management and foreign languages for business use.

Private tutors can command fees of from $10 to $20 per lesson. This doesn't mean you'll be earning $20 an hour for tutoring, because you must take into account a certain amount of time for lesson preparation and correcting homework. But with steady work, say ten or more students a week, you can earn a very nice supplemental income. Tutoring can be arranged for evening and weekend hours, while you work at a regular job during the business day.

The basic prerequisite for this business, of course, is that you know your subject well. You can purchase textbooks in any area in which you tutor. You must be sure that you know the needs of your student. If you are tutoring a public school student who is bed-ridden for a period of time, visit the student's regular teacher and make sure you are coordinating your efforts with the child's regular classroom curriculum.

Advertise your service in the local newspaper, being sure to specify the particular subjects in which you specialize. If you tutor adults in special skills, advertise also in any trade journals that relate to your subject. Place notices on college and school bulletin boards, and register with school authorities so that they may refer students to you who may need help.

89 · Recreation Area Concession

Beaches, stadiums, parks and picnic grounds are all fertile areas for successful concessions. What can you sell? Everything from hot dogs, coffee, soda, french fries and other foods to items that sell particularly at sporting events, like peanuts, hats, programs. At beaches and summer recreation events you can rent umbrellas, sun visors, even rubber floats.

To acquire concession rights to beaches, athletic events and other areas where the public congregates, you must come to an agreement with the sponsors of the events or the owners of the stadium or auditorium. These rights are usually exchanged for a percentage of gross receipts (anything from 25 percent on up). And that is probably the most difficult aspect of starting this business.

If you want to begin a concession business, make your arrangements for concession rights as early as possible—even as early as the season one year before the time you are contracting for. Once you have made satisfactory arrangements you can devote the interval to lining up supplies and part-time help.

The profit potential of a concessionaire is substantial. If you will be working a well-populated beach in the summertime, or a popular high school athletic schedule in other seasons, you will have virtually thousands of customers. You must plan your purchase of supplies carefully. Running short is an unforgivable error. Not only do you lose valuable profits, but you make a good case for losing your concession rights if it happens too often. Short of an outrageous miscalculation, it's almost impossible to overstock a concession. Leftover food can usually be frozen to preserve it for future use.

You may have noticed when purchasing food and sundries at a beach or football game that the prices were 30 percent to 50 percent higher than almost anyplace else outside the vicinity of the concession area. It's no accident that goods are overpriced. Concessionaires have a captive audience in most cases, and full advantage is taken of that situation. So, even with a percentage of gross receipts going toward "rental" of concession rights, you have a higher profit-per-item margin in this business than in most other retail sales. The mark-up on food and nonfood items can be three or four times the cost of the food.

Sellers of concession goods, if they are youngsters or others who hawk goods at a ball game, usually are paid a small percentage of their gross receipts. Thus, you can figure in advance exactly how much of your sales price for each item goes toward salespersons' commissions, as well as a fixed percentage for concession rights.

You can supplement beach and stadium concession income by selling food and souvenirs at public parades, carnivals, flea markets and other outdoor gatherings. Check local authorities for any licensing regulations that may prevail in your community.

90 · Custom Picture Framing

If you are a fair hand at carpentering, you can put yourself in a business that has a unique advantage over most businesses based on wood construction. Picture frames enjoy a high mark-up compared to almost all other types of wood and metal small products. Frames with materials costing no more than $5 can sell for $30 or more.

The reason is that people pay handsome sums of money for the hand-worked detail that goes into picture framing. For wood frames you would acquire a number of standard lengths of molding (the same kind used as ceiling and floor molding in homes). Metal stripping is also a popular component of many picture frames, and these can be purchased in precut lengths, ready to frame. You must also acquire sheets of glass, used in frames for prints, photographs and drawings. Learning to cut glass is not difficult, but it does require practice and a "feel," to become adept.

The tools necessary for this business are minimal: small hammer, drill, screwdrivers, small saws, miter box and mat knife, plus an assortment of screws and nails. A miter box will be one of your most valuable tools. This is the "form" you use to cut ends of wood at a 45 degree angle. In addition to wood strippings, metal strips and glass, you will also need a supply of construction cardboard which you use to create mats for photos and illustrations.

To learn the tricks in the art of framing, you can do no better than to work for an existing frame studio. You'll find that, like other crafts, picture framing can be learned by anyone with good dexterity. The quality that separates superior picture framers from others is the amount of creative imagination you can add to your craft. A sense of shapes and design, an ability to help your client select a frame that complements the work of art to be framed, will to a great extent determine how successful you can become.

You can operate your frame business from your home workshop. Customers can visit you at your shop, or you can carry sample corners of frames to your prospective clients' homes. A willingness on your part to travel to a client's home will give you an edge in advising how a particular frame will look in the setting the client has chosen to hang the picture.

Advertise your service in the newspaper and take a listing in the Yellow Pages. Also make a point of getting to know many interior decorators in your area. They are frequently called on to suggest types and makers of frames to their clients. Leave a supply of your business cards with portrait photographers, furniture and accessory retail merchants and anyone else who may be in a position to suggest a picture-framing service to a customer, even sellers of inexpensive prints. It is not at all unusual for a frame to cost three, four or ten times the cost of the item to be framed. Besides the actual framing, you will also be engaged to mount items, such as coins, bric-a-brac and three-dimensional mementos.

This is another of those businesses that lend themselves to evening and weekend work at the beginning. For people who have been engaged in woodworking as a hobby, it is a perfect opportunity to turn that weekend diversion into a truly lucrative business.

Experienced picture framers can turn a profit of $20,000 a year or more. By tracking the competition in your area, you'll get an idea of the pricing for picture frames. It's a high-profit business, especially if the framer becomes an artist in his own right.

91 · Idea Merchant

Here is a business in which you stock no inventory, deliver no products and have almost no overhead. Yet, it is a business in which you can gross over $50,000 a year.

Millions of people dream up good, solid, money-making ideas every year, but very few of those ideas ever go beyond the "gee whiz" stage. Why? Because very few people know how to translate those ideas into reality, or money. With a little effort, though, and a lot of perseverance, brilliant notions can turn to profit—and you can be the instrument of that profit, as well as one of the recipients.

As an idea merchant, it is your job to take concepts and sell them to those who *can* use them. If you see something in a store that can be improved, such as the idea one young man from Iowa had a few years back, you can make a tidy sum just for knowing where that idea can be sold and selling it. A man from Des Moines was browsing through a lamp store one day, trying to find an attractive floor lamp for his newly furnished apartment. The lamp he finally decided to buy was sleek and fashionable. There was only one problem. The switch was hard to reach. The lamp had a tall shade and he had to get way up under it to turn the switch. He bought the lamp anyway, took it home and began to think. He was sitting in an easy chair next to the lamp and he thought how easy it would be to turn the lamp on and off with a foot switch, a button on the floor that he could step on without even getting up from his chair. The next day he went to an electrical supply store and purchased a sturdy switch. He spliced this push-button switch into the lamp cord, placed the switch on the floor, and lo and behold, all he had to do was extend his leg slightly and he made that lamp much more convenient to use.

The next day he wrote to the manufacturer of the lamp, stating that he had found a way to improve their product greatly. Not only that, he also said he had been in touch with his attorney and had decided to patent his idea. Two days later he received a phone call from an executive of the lamp company. Would he be interested in selling his idea, the executive asked. Sure.

The end result was a check for $5000 from the lamp company to this young entrepreneur.

Now, all idea sales will not happen so fortuitously, nor will they be sold with such ease. But you'll never know for sure until you try it yourself. Almost everyone has come up with a way to improve some product in his home. Most human beings have extraordinary ingenuity when put to the test.

To make a business from the sale of ideas means more effort than just waiting for a good idea to strike. You have to advertise so that others will send their ideas to you. Running a small ad asking for people to send their ideas for new products, improvements on existing products, and fresh concepts will bring you a supply of mail that may be brimming with exciting concepts. You may have to reject most of them as unworkable, but if you come across an idea that looks promising, start getting in touch with manufacturers who might put that idea to use within the framework of the products they produce. If the idea is sold, you share the money earned from that concept with the originator, the person who sent it to you in the first place.

There are some precautions you must take first. Contact an attorney, preferably a patent attorney, and have a sample agreement drawn up that you will use to make an arrangement with people who submit ideas to you. This agreement will call for a specific split in any monies generated as a result of this idea, usually 50-50 between you, the merchandiser of the concept, and the originator. Also contained in this agreement will be a clause giving you exclusive rights to market the idea for a specific period of time, say two years. Next, you will have your attorney draw up an agreement that will be signed by those to whom you send the idea for consideration. This agreement will protect you from being exploited by a manufacturer who sees the idea, likes it, and decides to put it into effect without ever notifying you.

Once you have these protective agreements, your business success will be limited only by the creative imagination you exercise, and the perseverance with which you promote ideas in your possession. The profit potential is nearly limitless. One sold idea could net you thousands of dollars, enough to live on for a year, even if you don't sell another thing!

92 · Specialty Advertising Agency

One of the problems of many small businesses, whether a retail operation, manufacturer, or seller of services, is getting professional help in advertising. Because most advertising agencies can only afford to cater to accounts with multithousand-dollar ad budgets, small businesses have to rely on local newspapers to help them with their advertising needs. But the newspapers only perform this service as a way of stimulating advertising sales. They are, after all, in the publishing business and would probably be the first to admit that their advertising advice is little better than amateur.

If you've worked for an ad agency, or you've been part of the advertising and promotion service of a large company, or even if you've written public relations news releases, you could fill a small-business need that could provide you with a very nice income.

As an advertising service to small business, your chief asset (to the small business) is your price. But as an individual, with your own small business, you will be able to keep a very low overhead, and you will be able to charge for your services much more flexibly than a large ad agency. Your job will be to write copy, do layouts and suggest media to small businesses, all for a fee that they can afford. You can do this by charging an hourly rate for your services (rather than the 15 percent of money spent in advertising media, as large agencies charge). In essence, you will be what is known in the ad business as a one-man (or one-woman) shop.

Solicit accounts from your immediate area. Visit retail shops, small manufacturers, small service companies, and get them to try your service on a trial basis. Offer to prepare one promotion for them at nearly rock-bottom costs. Charge for your service at the rate of about $5 an hour, plus the cost of materials. Work out of your home. Limit your initial overhead to a small supply of stationery, business cards and envelopes. Try a small classified ad to draw inquiries, which should lead to personal interviews, and take a listing in the Yellow Pages as an ad agency catering specifically to small businesses. Put together a "portfolio" of your work, either work you've done in the past for an agency where you may have been employed, or sample layout and copy that you prepare especially for your portfolio.

Work closely with local newspapers and local, small-job printers. Both will be very cooperative because you represent a good source of business. Newspapers will frequently set type to your specifications, free, if that type is to be used in an ad that will appear in the newspaper.

The service you provide to your clients will be nearly invaluable. They will be getting professional advertising help at costs far below what a large agency would have to charge. As long as you keep your overhead to a minimum, by using outside services only as needed, you will be offering unbeatable prices. Despite the close-to-the-vest operation you are running, you can turn a handsome profit. You can net $200 a week or more very shortly after starting in business. As your agency grows, you'll find that newspapers, printers and even satisfied clients will refer other clients to you. As long as you maintain your personal service, even if your business starts to use a hired staff, you will remain successful. As a small-business specialist, you have a market that has barely been tapped.

93 · Custom T-Shirt Manufacturing

One of the biggest fashion explosions in years has been the appearance of decorated, lettered custom T-shirts. They are being worn by everyone from women's softball teams to diners at exclusive restaurants. With a minimum of supplies you can benefit from this fashion bonanza, and you can do it right from your home.

The first thing you need is a supply, as many as a gross (144), of assorted sizes of plain T-shirts. These can be ordered directly from manufacturers like Hanes, by mail. T-shirts are available in varying qualities. The best way to order would be to write to a manufacturer and ask for either a catalog or a description of available materials, and prices. In gross quantities, T-shirts can be purchased for less than 50¢ each, but you should make sure that the kind you order are of good quality and will not begin to unravel after one washing.

Next, you must acquire decorative stencils, non-water-soluble paints, sequins, felt transfer letters and designs—and you are ready to produce your creations. Take a tour of local clothing outlets and read several fashion magazines to get an idea of the kinds of decorated T-shirts that are most popular. But don't be limited just by what you see others making and wearing. The key to success in this business will be the originality and appeal of your own designs.

If you've purchased decent quality white T-shirts (which should be of the preshrunk variety), you can dye them with permanent color as step one. Colored T-shirts, with or without fancy designs, will always sell more readily than plain white. Paint or silk-screen lettering or designs of your choice. If you want to add handwork with stitching, sequins, studs, or wherever your imagination takes you, you can command higher prices. But the more handwork, the longer it will take to produce a finished shirt.

Take samples around to various retail outlets in your area. If merchants find your designs as appealing as you think they are, your T-shirts may be purchased on the spot. Boutiques, Army/Navy stores, even fancy dress shops are all good potential marketplaces for your shirts. Offer a personalizing service as part of a custom-order business.

Advertise directly to consumers in your local newspaper. Give people a reason to want your T-shirts by mentioning their possible uses specifically, such as team shirts for local amateur basketball, softball and tennis teams. Talk to local haircutters, plant shop owners and other local merchants who might want their store names on T-shirts, which they can then sell as novelty items to their customers —each one of whom is a potential walking advertisement. Mention to customers in your ads that these T-shirts make great party favors and unique gifts.

For a T-shirt that costs you 75¢ in materials, including decoration, and takes you fifteen minutes to manufacture, you can ask $3, $4, $5 or more. Sell a hundred T-shirts a week, and you can net $400 or more!

94 · Store Window Displays

If you have a sense of design, an artistic flair and a basic ability to create things with your hands, designing windows and interior store displays could become an excellent source of income. Any courses you may have had in graphic design, textiles, fashion, even art appreciation, will stand you in good stead. A visit to the library will provide you with several books on display techniques, and if you're really in need of training you can inquire at local schools about courses in design and display.

Window design and interior displays are basic three-dimensional tableaux, with the obvious purpose of showing off a store's products to good advantage. Display techniques depend as much on imagination and creative energy as they do on technical precision. One of the best ways to learn, of course, is to tour store windows in your community. You'll see some that are more appealing than others. Peer into the windows closely and see just what it is that makes some windows jump with life, while others look like the clothing was dropped by somebody walking through the display. It may be the lighting or the position of a mannequin or any of a dozen other details that makes the difference between appeal and turn-off.

The materials for displays are whatever strikes your fancy. Many window designs have been beautified by an old trunk from somebody's attic. Your tools to create designs are basic—a staple gun, hammer and nails, tissue paper, flameproof colored cardboard, plastics, glue, wire, paints, wood and foil—and, of course, your client's products. An excellent source of trendy ideas is *Display World* magazine. If you can't find it at your local library, you can subscribe by writing to DISPLAY WORLD, 140 W. 57th St., New York, N.Y.

As you tour the store windows in your area, note which ones you think could use the most improvement. Then do some rough sketches of how you think they could be made to look better, and pay a visit to the stores when you've prepared some ideas. Frequently, store windows are done as an after-thought by a merchant who may have little idea of what to do. And you may be surprised to discover that one or more merchants only did the windows because there was no one else to decorate them.

Your list of potential clients is really quite long: clothing stores, gift shops, boutiques, department stores, banks, hotels, museums, display jobbers, ad agencies, photographers—all of these either use window displays themselves or have clients who do. Whenever you do a window design or interior display, be sure to take photographs of them. These will be the heart of your portfolio, the proof of your work.

Your fees should be based on an average rate of $5 an hour. Your time should include not only actual work on the display at the store, but the time needed to design and sketch the display and time needed to acquire materials. In any event, this fee is a basic rate. You'll be able to charge substantial sums for certain jobs, and as an artist your fee cannot be measured in time only.

95 · Private Brand Vitamin Sales

One of the highest-profit items for sale in drugstores, supermarkets and health-food stores is vitamins. One hundred 500 mg. tablets of Vitamin C can cost as little as $1 and sell for as much as $6 or $7. But despite the high prices the demand for vitamins of all types is on the rise. Health-conscious America devours millions of dollars of a variety of vitamins *every day*. There's a way to cash in on this megavitamin appetite, without risking a penny of investment.

At the library you'll find a directory of pharmaceutical companies, both the giants and the ones nobody's ever heard of. The Food and Drug Administration keeps a pretty close eye on all manufacturers of drugs, prescription and over-the-counter types. So a small drug manufacturer can be assumed to have products just as safe and pure as the big boys.

Write to one of these smaller manufacturers and ask for their catalog of vitamins. Explain to them that you are a private labeler of vitamin products and you want to consider that company as a potential supplier. Once you have received catalogs from two or more competitive manufacturers, you can begin sales of your private label vitamins.

There are two avenues you can travel to sell your product. One is to local drug and health-food stores that would like to stock vitamins with the store's name on the label. People who frequent these local stores will expect that store-name brands will be less expensive than the major pharmaceutical brands, and they'll be right. You can sell to several competitive drugstores in the same community, because they'll each be stocking their own private brand names. Your profit on these commercial sales will be probably equal to your cost for the vitamins. Offer to design and print the store's own brand labels, which you will apply directly to the bottles of vitamins you receive from the manufacturer.

The other sales outlet you can exploit is direct selling to the consumer. Test one or two small ads, both in local newspapers and in national publications. Give your own name to the vitamins you sell by this method, and print and apply your own labels. Advertise reduced prices and stress that these are private brand products, conforming to all government regulations, and that they are available at special low prices. With retail sales by you to the consumer, even if you take something less than a five-time mark-up, you can profit handsomely.

Vitamins are considered nutrients, not medicine. Therefore, they can be marketed without a prescription and can be purchased in any quantity.

By combining wholesale distribution and direct retail sales by mail, you can profit two ways in a market that shows no sign of shrinking. On the contrary, vitamins are selling at a greater rate than ever. Your profit as a one-person business in this "growth field" can soar to $100,000 or more a year, and you need not purchase from a manufacturer until after you have a sales commitment from local retail outlets.

96 · Window Washing Service

If you've ever driven through your downtown area early in the morning, before the business day has begun, you've seen them with their squeegees and buckets laboriously cleaning large display windows on every store in the area. It's not fancy work, but it's a remarkably lucrative service that can pay you the equivalent of $12 an hour! Window washing? Yes, cleaning windows, inside and out, with a swipe of the hand.

You can get into this lucrative service businesss with virtually no investment, and you'll have an opportunity to make it pay surprisingly well. The only secret to profitable window washing is efficiency. A 6 foot by 9 foot pane of glass can be washed on two sides in eight to twelve minutes. A contract to clean a window that size, once a week, can bring you $8 a month. Not much by itself, but line up 30, 50 or 100 contracts like that and you can see how quickly those dollars multiply.

Window washing services are highly competitive. It's a skill that can be taught in a few minutes. And the investment in supplies is about $2 per window washer. If you clean windows yourself, as well as line up your own clients, you can net several hundred dollars a month working *part time!* It's a business that can be started and operated while you hold a regular day job, because by necessity window washing is done early in the morning (during daylight), before stores open.

Advertise your window washing service in the classified section of your newspaper, and take a listing in the Yellow Pages. But don't count on clients to come running to their phones to call you. Chances are, most stores and offices already use a window washing service. So, if you want business, you're going to have to go out there personally and drum it up.

To get someone to switch services is difficult, but it can be done, even if the service a potential client now uses is quite satisfactory. The trick is to make an offer that even the most hard-nosed business person will find almost impossible to turn down.

You might, for instance, offer free service for the first month of a contract. It means you might be working for everyone for nothing during that month, but it will pay in the long run if you can lock up a one-year contract as a result. You can also try the free gift route —fresh flowers delivered once a week, free, when you wash the client's windows. Or, an agreement to wash a merchant's windows at his home, free, one time in return for a contract to do the store windows. There are ways when you become determined. They are not unethical (even to your window-washing competitors). It's just a matter of aggressive business solicitation.

One office-building contract can net you several hundred dollars a month alone. And you can hire a staff of window washers at reasonable salaries—even part-time help for early morning work. In addition to contract work for businesses, you can offer a home window washing service on a one-time basis. In this case, you visit a home and make careful estimates of the time needed to do all the windows. This kind of service pays better on a per-window basis, but cannot be counted on, usually, for more than once-a-month business. The advantage to residential window cleaning is that it can be done during the business day, when merchants would prefer *not* to have window washers standing in front of their displays.

97 · Organic Produce Sales

The more we learn about food additives, chemical preservatives and insecticides, the more depressed we seem to get concerning what we ingest every day. More and more Americans are turning to healthy (not just health) foods every day. The problem with organic vegetables is that they are more difficult to grow than vegetables treated with chemicals. The huge "industrial" farms have spurned this method because it cuts too deeply into their mass production schedule.

But thousands of small farmers *are* growing organic vegetables, and you can become one by using the vegetable garden right on your own property. The market for these organically grown vegetables is substantial, in community health food stores or even right at your own roadside stand.

Organic gardening is based on little or no use of chemical fertilizers and insecticides. That doesn't mean your plants don't get any fertilizer. The difference is that you use organic matter instead of chemicals. Natural compost provides fertilizer, and selected flowers and plants that discourage insects are your natural insecticide.

Composting is simply the recycling of waste back into the land. To prepare a compost pile, you need a plastic-lined garbage can to which you add a proportion of grass cuttings, dead leaves and kitchen (food) garbage, plus manure to speed up the deterioration process. Keep the garbage can covered with a tight lid, and you have a natural fertilizer factory right in your own yard.

By planting certain flowers, like marigolds, around the circumference of your garden you have a natural barrier to plant-eating insects. A good book to read on this subject is *Companion Plants and How to Grow Them*, probably available at your library. Another good source of information is the monthly magazine called *The Organic Gardener*.

When you're ready to harvest your crop, you simply wash the vegetables well to eliminate any clinging insects. If you've planted a vegetable garden before, you already have a basic familiarity with your growing season and yields. Organic gardening is slightly more time-consuming, but when you sell your produce, you'll get more money and you'll be providing vegetables that taste and look considerably better than commercially available produce.

When you've harvested your crop, sell as much as possible to area health food stores. They will be a good outlet but will only take a limited quantity, due to the refrigeration needs of fresh food. Also open your own organic vegetable stand, which is simply a couple of boards stretched across two barrels, with produce containers piled around them. You can also load up a station wagon or pickup truck and drive from community to community, selling right off the back of your vehicle. A large cardboard sign with the words ORGANIC VEGETABLES—PICKED FRESH in big letters.

Even though you'll be able to command prices up to 30 percent or more higher than your local supermarket, your own yield of vegetables will not provide an income for you to sit back until the next growing season. If you have friends or neighbors who also grow organic vegetables, you can buy their whole crop, add it to your own, and increase the inventory substantially that you take around in your vehicle.

This business is obviously not a full-time venture, unless you're farming many acres. It is a way, however, to turn a recreational vegetable garden into a valuable cash crop—worth perhaps several hundred dollars to you, in addition to the fresh groceries you provide, free, for your family.

98 · Jewelry Design and Repair

Even with the inflationary rise in the prices of gold, silver and precious stones, there is a vast market for custom-designed jewelry in which the profits far exceed the simple value of the components. The reason, of course, is that custom-jewelry design and execution is an art—one that can be learned and improved on quickly, but an art nevertheless.

If you have a reasonable degree of dexterity, if your fingers are agile enough to handle tweezers, small pliers and miniature settings, you can craft your own jewelry and enjoy a good income from sales of your product.

Gold, silver and stones of all types are readily available from either wholesale supply houses or even many hobby shops. And in certain parts of the country, silver especially can be purchased at relatively low prices. To begin, you'll need a basic supply of jewelry components—beads, liquid silver and small stones for necklaces; precious and semiprecious stones, like jade and opal, for rings and pins; gold and silver settings, and anything else that your creative imagination can apply to custom jewelry (even colorful feathers!).

You should also pay a visit to the library and read one or more books on jewelry design. If you can take a course in custom jewelry making, perhaps being offered by a craftsperson in your area, so much the better.

Once you have acquired your supplies, and the basic skill to use them, you're ready to go into business. You'll probably find that necklaces are the easiest jewelry to create. The way you design the series of beads, liquid silver and other items you string will determine the appeal of the necklace. It's the choice of colors and materials that makes the difference. The beading, or stringing, is relatively simple.

Take several samples of your work to local gift shops, as well as small specialty stores selling men's and women's apparel and accessories. If you bring your jewelry ready to display, you'll be making it much more convenient for the store to sell your product. Pieces of driftwood with jewelry placed on the branches are an extremely attractive setting. Give some thought to the display before taking your jewelry around. Even a piece of dark velvet stapled to a small board is an attractive display, and it takes only a few minutes to make. Your wholesale price to merchants either willing to buy or take jewelry on consignment should represent at least twice the actual cost of your materials. For rings, pins and other items in which you have put many hours of labor, you should be compensated at the rate of at least $5 an hour, plus the cost of the materials. Some items will bring you even ten times your cost, but you will have to determine the best price to ask after you have done some competitive shopping in your area.

Advertise your custom jewelry and repair service in the classified section of the newspaper and in the Yellow Pages. If merchants selling your jewelry are willing, also place a card advertising your service near the displays you have set up in various retail outlets. People looking at your work may not see an item they want, but they will be able to look at this work as samples and might be stimulated to ask for a custom creation (or repair) based on what they've seen.

Fees for jewelry repair should be set at a rate of $5 an hour. If you can estimate how long it will take to effect a repair, then give estimates to your customers. If it looks impossible to determine exactly how much time it will take, make sure you're at least covered for a minimum number of hours. If you are willing to pay a commission to retail merchants for custom sales and repair sent through them, you will probably have little difficulty in getting them to place a small sign near your jewelry display.

Many custom jewelry designers have started in a home workshop and have seen their business grow to the point where it made sense to open a retail outlet. The point is that you can clear $15,000 a year or more from this business, starting with less than $100 worth of components, and no other overhead.

99 · Home Service Registry

One of the problems facing most small service businesses is the time it takes to drum up business. Home repair specialists, painters, floor refinishers, even babysitters, all complain that they spend half their time looking for work and the other half doing it. An answer to this problem, and a business itself, is a clearinghouse which keeps a list of home service people. The clearinghouse, or registry, solicits those who need anything done in or around the home, calls in a carpenter or babysitter at the request of a customer, and collects a fee for performing this valuable function. The fee can be anything from 10 percent of the gross receipts for a job (collected from the painter, refinisher, etc., who gets the work) to a flat fee for registering the service person, plus a fee for work received as a result of the effort of the clearinghouse.

To start your own service registry, first get in touch with as many reliable carpenters, electricians, plumbers, floor sanders, babysitters and others as you can. Most will willingly pay a small registration fee of from $10 to $50 (or even a monthly rate of, say, $5) to be listed by your registry.

Then you advertise for home customers. One classified ad in a regional magazine went something like this: "Full Service Registry —Carpenters, Painters, Floor Sanders, Plumbers, Movers, Cleaners, Babysitters. 7 Days, 9 A.M.-10 P.M. Call 295-9066." Simple, but effective. This registry received dozens of calls from this one ad.

The key to your success will be the reliability of your service personnel. Check references, call others for whom work was done, and check on the satisfaction of customers served by your contracted services.

To start this business you need never leave your home. You can solicit service people and answer calls from prospective customers right from your own phone. If your service proves satisfactory to both workers and customers, you will get a great deal of repeat business. As much of a problem as it is for service businesses to get work, it's almost as difficult for home and apartment dwellers to find reliable businesses to call. Once you establish a reputation for providing good workers at reasonable prices, you'll be relied on more and more heavily.

When people call for services, you must be prepared to quote general rates on the telephone. State, for instance, that your carpenters get $6 an hour, your babysitters get $1.50 an hour, and so on. Also stress to callers those services you didn't have room to list in your classified ads, such as bartenders for parties, guitarists to entertain at children's birthdays, messengers who will pick up groceries, and virtually any other service that relates to the home.

With a good supply of service people subscribing to your service, you could clear several hundred dollars a week without ever getting up from your chair.

100 · Christmas Corporate Gift Service

Can you imagine a business in which you earn more in sixteen weeks than most people earn in a year. The answer is a specialized holiday gift service. Every American knows that Christmas giving is a retailer's dream. Yet, less known is the gold mine in business gift-giving. According to *Incentive Marketing* magazine, corporate gift-giving will top the $400,000,000 (that's right, four hundred million dollars) mark this year. In fact, each year it gets bigger and bigger.

How can you cash in on the corporate Santa Claus? Easy, First identify a list of potential clients. Your local Yellow Pages should be a help. *Any* business that sells to other businesses is a hot prospect. On the list include the big gift users such as advertising agencies, insurance people, commercial printers and similar service firms. Avoid companies that only have a small commercial volume. For example, a dry cleaner may do corporate drapes, yet most of his business will be individuals.

Once armed with a list of potential buyers, fill out an index card with each name. Even in the smallest town it shouldn't be hard to come up with a hundred prospects. Remember everyone from plumbing supply firms to linen services are potentials.

Next, put together your line. You'll want items that wholesale for from $2 to $50. Most corporate gifts are in the $10 price range. You can do this by asking wholesalers what items are popular. Locate wholesalers by checking any big-city Yellow Pages. Some good corporate-type gifts are pens, scarves, cameras, wallets, radios, calculators and small appliances.

You'll want a line of both female and male gifts. However, stay away from items in which sizes are important.

Buy a sample of each item or if possible simply take a catalog sheet on each item you select.

Now you're in business! Visit each prospect on your list. In small companies ask to see the president, in bigger companies ask to see the marketing director.

Your sales pitch should be something like this: "Hi, my name is Fred Schultz and I'm with Schultz Gift Company. If you plan to give

Christmas gifts to your employees or clients this year I can help you. You see, Mr. Smith, we offer a selection of gifts with no shopping problems. We'll even gift-wrap your selection, put in a card, and deliver or mail it. What could be a simpler way to shop?"

Then show him your samples or catalog sheets.

In figuring prices add about 25 percent to your cost. For example, an item that costs you $10 should be sold at $12.50. Also charge $1 a gift for wrapping. A service of this type can absorb the delivery cost if deliveries are all in one downtown area. On parcel post orders we suggest you charge a mailing fee of $1 per package plus actual postage and insurance.

Start selling by October 15th. Businessmen (unlike consumers) plan their Christmas gifts early. If you're mailing gifts, get them all to the post office by December 10th. Also sell on a COD basis. Avoid costly collection problems. Most wholesalers will let you buy as needed. Therefore you won't be laying out a lot of cash.

This is no small-time business if you hit a few good accounts. One plastics company we know sends out over a thousand Christmas gifts every year. Imagine the profit on a single order like that!

The key here is start early and work hard. You only have a few months to earn a year's profits!